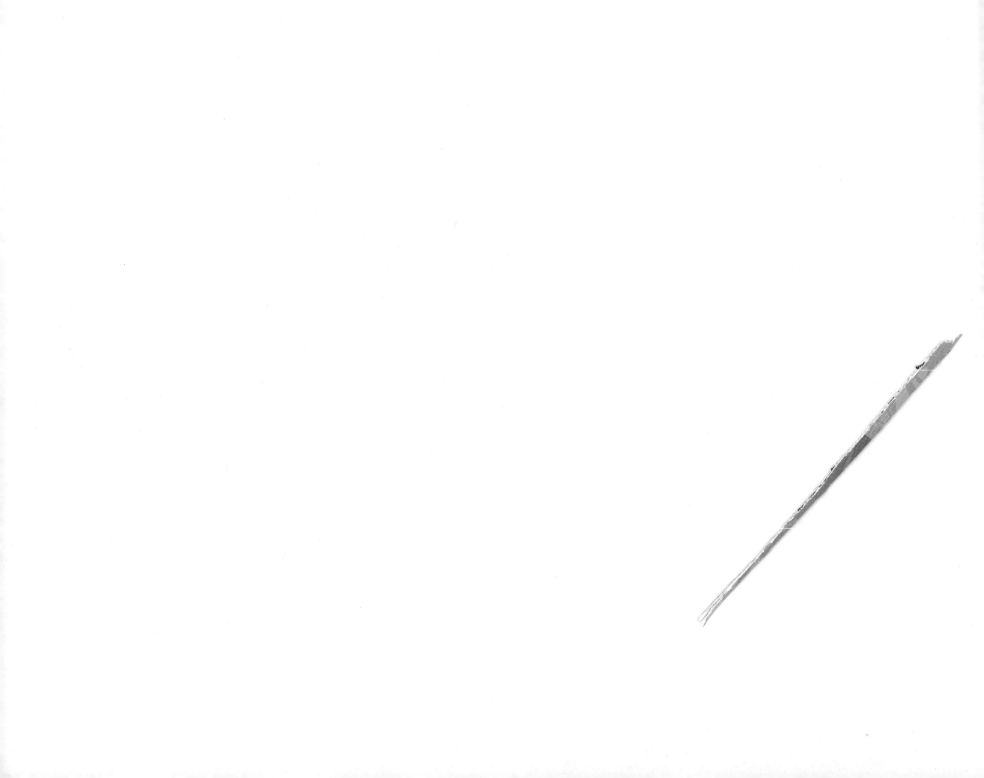

A COMMEMORATIVE EDITION ON

THE NINETIETH ANNIVERSARY OF

THE BATTLE OF THE SOMME

1 JULY TO 18 NOVEMBER, 1916

LONDON, NEW YORK,
MUNICH, MELBOURNE, DELHI

DORLING KINDERSLEY
Managing Editor Debra Wolter
Managing Art Editor Karen Self
Publisher Jonathan Metcalf
Production Controller Jo Bull
DTP Designer John Goldsmid

Book and film produced for Dorling Kindersley by M2

71 Leonard Street, London EC2A 4QU
duncan@mtwo.co.uk / david@mtwo.co.uk

Designers
Duncan Youel, David Edgell, Philippa Baile,
Lynnette Eve, Kate Stretton and Gill Patchett

Editor
Andrew Heritage

Historical Consultant
Michael Stedman

Photography
Keith Lillis, Michael Stedman, M2 Archive

First published in the United States by DK Publishing, Inc.
375 Hudson Street, New York, New York 10014

A Penguin Company

00 01 02 03 04 05 10 9 8 7 6 5 4 3 2 1

ISBN 13: 978-0-75662-477-4
ISBN 10: 0-7566-2477-0

Printed and bound in the UK by Printwright, Ipswich.

Discover more at
www.dk.com

For more information about M2 visit www.mtwo.co.uk

THE SOMME

THEN AND NOW – A VISUAL HISTORY

DUNCAN YOUEL AND DAVID EDGELL

Our gratitude and thanks to His Royal Highness The Prince of Wales,
Tim Gregson, Andrew Heritage, Michael and Yvonne Stedman, Keith
Lillis, Sir Frank Sanderson, Piers Storie-Pugh, Sir Evelyn Webb-Carter,
Guillaume de Fonclare, Rod and Jackie Bedford, Dominique Zanardi,
ms. Arlene King, Philippe and Mme Feret, Teddy and Phoebe Colligan,
Mme Potie, Liz Bower, the Imperial War Museum, Sian Mexsom, the
Army Benevolent Fund, Peter Francis, the Commonwealth War Graves
Commission, Grant Wright, Patrick Roberts, Lianne Knights and staff
at Printwright in Ipswich.

Dedicated to Tom Youel and Felix Edgell, the next generation;
and to Philippa Baile and Maria Edgell.

And for David Youel, 26 November 1961 to 6 March 2005. Rest in peace.

CONTENTS

CONTENTS

CONTENTS

HRH PRINCE OF WALES

I am extremely grateful for this opportunity to contribute my thoughts to this book which commemorates the 90th anniversary of the Battle of the Somme. The magnitude of our losses on 1st July 1916 caused a profound shock to the nation at the time and the scars remain with us today. It was not just the sheer scale of our losses, fifty thousand casualties in one day, of which 20,000 were killed (or missing, presumed dead), it was also the fact that for the first time in our history, we committed a citizen army to the assault. Thus it was that hundreds of friends and colleagues, who had volunteered together from factories and tram works and coal mines, to form battalions of Pals, went over the top together and died together, often before they could reach the enemy trenches. Many villages and towns lost an entire generation of their menfolk – their sons, brothers, husbands and fathers – in one terrible day. There are monuments to their memory throughout the United Kingdom and their headstones, in hundreds of cemeteries across the Somme, are a testament to their sacrifice; the Thiepval monument alone bears the names of more than 72,000 British and Commonwealth soldiers who remain missing from that battle.

Sadly, there are very few surviving veterans of the First World War alive today. However, the story of their suffering, tenacity and courage lives on – not just on Remembrance Day and through many other ceremonies, but also as part of our educational curriculum. More school children visit the battlefields of Northern France today than ever before. The legend of "Tommy Atkins" is a firm part of our national self-image. We will remember him.

This book is a welcome addition to the story of the Battle of the Somme. It is primarily pictorial history, juxtaposing archive and contemporary material, and it is part documentary, part travelogue. It gives the reader a clear orientation to the battlefields and connects them with villages and towns back home, so that it is very much easier to locate the places where our forebears fought, and died, on the Somme. I am delighted that part of the proceeds from the sale of this book will go to the Army Benevolent Fund, which was established by my Grandfather, King George VI, in 1945. The need for the A.B.F., for the welfare of our soldiers, serving and retired, and their families, continues to this day.

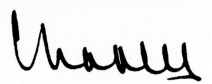

TIM GREGSON

BRIGADIER TIM GREGSON, MBE, MILITARY ATTACHÉ, PARIS – AND COLONEL OF THE DURHAM LIGHT INFANTRY.

As the British Military Attaché based in the Embassy in Paris, I pay several visits to the Somme each year. Often I take part in commemorations, such as our own at Thiepval and the Ulster Tower on 1st July each year – and those of our Commonwealth allies, such as the Australian ceremony at Villers-Bretonneux in April, or the South African ceremony at Delville Wood later on in July. I also come to the Somme several times a year to help re-inter British soldiers whose remains have been discovered in the fields surrounding the front line. In nearly all cases, ninety years after the battle, the identity of these soldiers is unknown; and there is no family or regiment to honour them. So, together with a small team from the Commonwealth War Graves Commission and a Padre, I help bury those remains, lay a wreath and salute their sacrifice.

I am a Light Infantryman and my father was a Durham Light Infantryman. On the eastern extremity of the Somme battlefield, several miles behind the German front line on 1 July, there is a small pimple on the landscape called the Butte de Warlencourt. This was the scene of some of the most bitter fighting of the battle, because its comparative height made it a perfect observation post for Forward Observation Officers of the German artillery, who used it to telling effect. In early November (towards the end of the battle), 151st Durham Brigade was ordered to attack. The Brigade comprised three battalions: 6DLI, 8DLI and 9DLI. The latter was commanded by one of the most remarkable leaders of the entire war: Lt Col Roland Boys Bradford. He was 24 years old at the time.

The attack began on 5 November, an iconic day in the DLI calendar because it is Inkerman Day, celebrating the Crimean battle in which the Serjeants of the Regiment carried the day, all their officers having been killed (hence we continue to wear the Inkerman Whistle and Chain on our cross belts to this day).

On 5 November 1916 the weather was terrible and the Durhams advanced knee deep in mud. Inevitably, perhaps, our preliminary artillery barrage had failed to destroy the German positions and they were waiting for us with their own artillery and machine guns. Before long 6DLI and 8DLI were ground to a halt – but amazingly 9 DLI not only took the Butte but also advanced well beyond it. Unfortunately, they remained un-reinforced and isolated. Taking heavy casualties and pressed by continuous German counter attacks, Colonel Bradford was forced to withdraw. The Brigade had suffered over 1,000 casualties without gain. 9DLI alone lost 17 officers killed, wounded or missing; and 30 other ranks dead, 250 wounded and 111 missing, presumed dead (over 400 casualties in that one battalion).

This story reminds me of the terrible cost of the Somme and the sacrifice of a generation. Families that never saw their sons, their brothers, husbands and fathers again. But it also reminds me of the fighting spirit, the tenacity and raw courage of British soldiers in adversity – and it makes me very proud of my Regiment, The Light Infantry.

This book marks the 90th anniversary of the Battle of the Somme. By using historical and contemporary images it attempts to bridge the gap between the tragic events of 1916 and today. It is a souvenir to accompany the many ceremonies, grand and small, that will take place in every corner of the battlefield this year. Whilst I have been privileged in helping to organize the very public Service of Remembrance at Thiepval on 1 July, I am very conscious that there will also be hundreds of private, family acts of remembrance in France and at home; and that this will continue for many generations to come.

We Will Remember Them.

SIR EVELYN WEBB-CARTER

MAJOR-GENERAL SIR EVELYN WEBB-CARTER KCVO OBE. CONTROLLER, ARMY BENEVOLENT FUND

For many military historians, the First World War represents the first major war of the industrial age. In military terms, it marked a transition in the way warfare was conducted, a move away from the dominant role of the cavalry to one that was increasingly mechanised. The range at which the conflict was fought also changed, and changes in technology meant that prolonged artillery bombardment at a distance became a feature of the Great War.

Somme 90 is a new telling of the Battle of the Somme and commemorates one of the most significant battles of the First World War, which took place during July - November 1916. The authors give a candid view of the operation, illustrated with both new and old materials. As a former soldier, I believe this book will help to inform the reader of the scale of the battle, and the impact that it had not only on the soldiers of the Allied and German armies but also on the communities in Picardy where the battle was fought. The photographs, both contemporary and recent, will also help to guide the reader through the main lines of the battle, including High Wood, one of the most significant operations during the Battle of the Somme.

In November 1918, at the end of the First World War, there was very little provision to assist soldiers who had been severely injured or families who faced hardship if their loved one had been killed. Several specialist charities were set up, such as St Dunstan's, Combat Stress and the Royal Star and Garter Home, all of which continue to provide excellent services for disabled former soldiers. Yet what help there was available was not sufficient to meet the needs of returning soldiers, such as helping them to find employment, or financial help to assist them live independently at home if they had become disabled as a result of their war service. As a result, many families suffered great financial hardship.

In the closing months of the Second World War, several senior soldiers who were themselves veterans of the First World War realised that returning soldiers from the then current period of conflict would require practical help. Under the patronage of King George VI they established the Army Benevolent Fund – the Army's national charity – to assist returning soldiers and their families. Since then, we have supported many thousands of soldiers, former soldiers and their families who are in real need as well as providing funding for a raft of smaller, specialist charities that work directly with the wider Army family.

The Army Benevolent Fund addresses five key areas of priority: to support those ex-soldiers who have become disabled or face infirmity as a result of old age; to assist ex-soldiers find alternative employment when they leave the Army; to help ex-soldiers who are experiencing homelessness; and to meet the needs of families of serving soldiers, in particular their children. Today, our practical help ranges from funding a specialist wheelchair for the disabled child of a serving soldier, mobility aids so that a Second World War veteran can continue to live independently at home, or a much-needed holiday for a war widow and her children. Until very recently, we had assisted many First World War veterans, including veterans of the Battle of the Somme. We work with veterans of every theatre of operation since the Second World War, including recent operations such as the Balkans, Northern Ireland, Iraq and Afghanistan.

The Army Benevolent Fund is pleased to have contributed in a small way to the production of the book on the Somme and is delighted to have been nominated as the charity to benefit from the book and accompanying DVD. This will help us to continue our important work with veterans of every campaign and theatre of operation since the First World War, including those on active service today.

PIERS STORIE-PUGH

MBE DL, FOUNDER AND HEAD OF REMEMBRANCE TRAVEL, THE ROYAL BRITISH LEGION

No battle it seems evokes such outrage and feeling as does the Somme of 1916 for it sucked thousands of young men into her bottomless pits. Coupled with the word Somme are such charges as incompetence, disloyalty, self-deception, poor leadership; to the extent that any outside reader could draw the conclusion that nothing whatsoever was gained by this battle which raged through 1916 and finally petered out in the bitter temperatures of November.

The Army of 1916 was a hotchpotch made up of the remnants of the Regular Army, soldiers of the Territorial Force, some conscripts, members of Kitchener's New Army and soldiers from the Empire. There is no doubt that the Army that was put into the Field in 1917 was far more professional in its field discipline and staff work than the one that entered the Battle of the Somme in 1916. If one believe this, or even only part of this, then the young men who fell in Picardy did not die in vain.

As early as 1915 the War Office was besieged and beseeched by relatives for news of those who had fallen. There was no good news to be had, for not only had they died, seemingly in vain, but no trace could be found and no record kept; until Fabian Ware established his remarkable work, now embodied internationally in the Commonwealth War Graves Commission based at Maidenhead, England. Its work is carried out in 143 different Countries but its origins are deeply entrenched on the Western Front. It is the outstanding work of this body, coupled with The Royal British Legion's Remembrance Travel that ensures that the memory of those who died is never forgotten, and that Remembrance is taken right into the field where they made the supreme sacrifice.

In 1927 the first ever Legion Pilgrimage got under way with 150 Pilgrims, en route to France to pay respects to those who had fallen, and to gain some idea of the appalling conditions in which the men had fought. This first Pilgrimage so fired the imagination of the Nation that the following year a staggering 10,000 Pilgrims set out for Belgium and France, their aim being 'to show to the World that their loved ones are not forgotten and above all that the purpose for which they died is still remembered. Prince and Ploughman, General and Private Soldier, Mother and Widow, found unity in something greater even than the discipline of War and on the very scenes of their kinsmen's sacrifice.'

Field Marshal Haig was to be on this pilgrimage but died en route, but not before this 'remote and uncaring' man had established the foundations of The Royal British Legion as a non-political and non-sectarian body whose role was to safeguard the interests and welfare of the ex-Service community and their dependants. That central theme has never changed. In 1985 the Government invited The Royal British Legion to set up an operation which would enable relatives to visit the graves of those who had fallen. This scheme included a grant in aid specifically for War Widows.

The ideals and principles established by our forefathers that there should be in place a Pilgrimage Scheme for relatives indeed remains in force; and even 90 years after that great watershed of a battle, The Somme, Pilgrims still make their way to this sacred place. They are continuing to do what the architects of the 1928 Pilgrimage had in mind 'that the purpose for which they died is still remembered!'

INTRODUCTION

From 2002 to 2005 M2 were responsible for producing the visual displays and films for the Thiepval Visitor Centre. During our research we had the pleasure and privilege of working alongside a number of academics, historians and enthusiasts. We have learned much and are indebted to Professor Peter Simkins, Brother Nigel Cave, Michael Stedman, Michael Barker and Sir Frank Sanderson.

The expansive education we have received over the past few years has brought home to us that there is no one definitive version of the cataclysm of ninety years ago. Moreover, there appears to be a multiplicity of views on the subject, and the natures of these views have changed over time too. Statistics, opinions and conjectures seem to circle the subject interminably, occasionally colliding. In attempting to resolve these anomalies we have, almost inadvertently, found ourselves sharing the commitment, enthusiasm and passion of those involved in Great War interpretation.

Having previously documented aspects of British culture, the prospect of addressing the Battle of the Somme – one of the cornerstone events of the 20th Century in many ways – and its perception today, in both book and film, was an irresistible challenge. We felt it demanded a different, fresh approach, which drew upon references as diverse as Sassoon to Dada, Nash to Sheriff, and Spiritualism to the Wall Street Crash and Hitler to Blackadder.

During the project we have observed various aspects of the Somme experience today, which range from the mannequins kitted out in Aussie uniform standing guard at Le Tommy bar in Pozieres, to the fortifications at the entrance to the glades of French academe at Peronne. In our opinion, both deserve equal scrutiny, to enable us to unravel the texture and fabric of the Somme today. This then, is a visual history which contextualises these and other locations with the scenes of ninety years ago.

We set out to produce an intelligent, engaging but above all accessible, guide to the history, geography and the modern experience of the Somme. It is our hope that the reader and viewer will be sufficiently enthused to explore the many sites that make up the battlefields and memorials. Ninety years on, the countryside has regained the picturesque charm it had held for many British soldiers upon their arrival in autumn 1915, although the hundreds of cemeteries and memorials that now punctuate this rural landscape are an ever-present reminder of the horrors which they were to endure in the following months.

We are privileged to mark the occasion of the ninetieth anniversary of the Battle of the Somme with this commemorative edition. It has been made possible by the overwhelming tide of goodwill and assistance from so many people, and in particular, Brigadier Tim Gregson, based at the British Embassy in Paris, whose encouragement and enthusiasm for the project has been invaluable.

Duncan Youel and David Edgell
May 2006

THE SOMME THEN

While this book concentrates on what is commonly referred to as the first battle of the Somme, which started on 1 July 1916 and lasted until 18 November of the same year, it is important to set this pivotal moment of the Great War of 1914-18 in its broader historical context.

In the following pages, the reasons why the Great War broke out, and the principal events which occurred up to the Summer of 1916 are summarized in pictures, captions and accompanying text. Similarly, pages 136-151, summarize the aftermath of the battle of the Somme, and the events leading to the Armistice in November 1918.

The 19th century had seen a transformation of the way in which the world worked. Three principal factors provided the motive forces for this change, and all sprang from Europe: the growth of empire; industrialization; and the impact of these on the European social structure.

The shift from mercantile colonialism to the establishment and consolidation of overseas empires, was led by Britain when it wrested control of the Indian sub-continent, Russia, which spread its direct control eastwards across Siberia to the Pacific, and France which, with Britain, carved up much of Africa between them in the last three decades of the century.

But, at the heart of Eurasia was the Turkish Ottoman empire, the "sick man of Europe", an imperial force which had come to prominence in the 15th century, and which was now in decline. It was not alone, for at the centre of Europe lay the Habsburg empire of Austria-Hungary – by 1900 tottering along on the twin crutches of aristocratic tradition and a glimpse of glorious expansion eastwards as Ottoman control of south-eastern Europe receded in the face of nationalism. Nationalism was rampant elsewhere in Europe at the time: newly independent states like Belgium appeared alongside a "reunified" Italy and Germany.

The Spithead Review in 1897, marking Queen Victoria's Diamond Jubilee, featured over 150 state-of-the-art vessels, and was a timely reminder of Britain's naval superiority and imperial outreach. Most of Victoria's various European royal relatives were invited to attend, among them Prince Henry of Prussia.

High jinks at the Henley Regatta. British society at the beginning of the 20th century was deeply class-riven, while the nation itself, ever-insular, regarded the threat of war "on the Continent" as at best a rather remote threat to its stability.

Across the Atlantic, in Latin America, the last colonial holdings of two other *ancien regimes*, Spain and Portugal, had been swept away in a tide of national independence; meanwhile, north of the Rio Grande the world's first modern democratic republic, the United States, following the civil war in the 1860s, was determined to plough its own furrow, whilst tending its "backyard". Despite occasional imperial adventures in Cuba, the Philippines and China, the US remained in principle isolationary. Nevertheless the young nation acted as a magnetic promised land for the 50 million or so Europeans and Asians who migrated there between 1800 and 1910.

The growth of the British, French and Russian empires had been underpinned by the Industrial Revolution. As new technologies developed, and wealth was created for the middle and working classes across Europe, so new markets expanded. These required an expanding resource-base, be it cotton from India, iron ore and coal from Siberia, precious metals from Africa, coffee, tea or rubber from plantations across the tropical belt.

Britain, France and the US seized and exploited the opportunities it offered, building canals, railways and steamships which brought the world's products to their door, and in turn exported their manufactured goods across the globe. Russia, by 1912 the world's third largest industrial power, embraced 'modernization' and wealth for the elite, whilst for the most part, aside from luxury trains and central heating, the advantages of industrialization largely passed Austria-Hungary and the Ottomans by. Germany, newly united under Bismarck, saw the opportunities, but with few colonies of any value – no "place in the sun" – the nation felt embittered, and focussed on building its infrastructure and armaments. By 1900 Germany was like a powder keg, ready to explode.

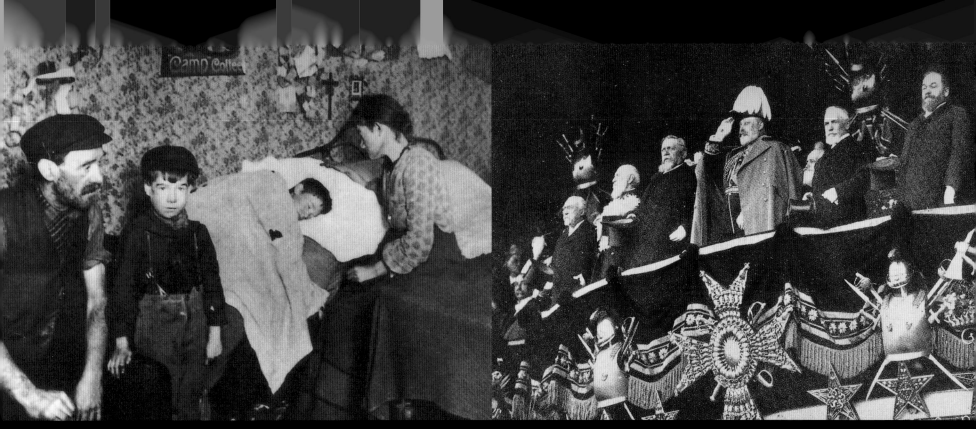

At the other end of the scale, there was a burgeoning urban underclass, living in hastily-built, slum conditions in cities throughout Great Britain. Despite initiatives in education and public health, their lot was dismal, although patriotism remained largely unquestioned.

King Edward VII attending a celebration in Paris to inaugurate the "Entente Cordiale". Always uneasy neighbours, and politically radically different, both France and Britain recognized the danger posed by a heavily-armed and belligerent Germany.

Another effect of the industrialization was the rapid growth of the urban population, largely the result of people migrating from the countryside to seemingly wealth-producing towns and cities. In the wake of this, proposals for social reform, universal education, social welfare, and political enfranchisement began to take root in a manner that the old ruling order found distinctly uncomfortable. The ideas of Marx and Engels concerning a new egalitarian socio-industrial ethic were a product of the times.

Again, the impact was geographically varied: Britons saw wealth flowing across its trans-global imperial holdings, then trickling down through its class structure – patriotism reached a crescendo in the latter decades of Queen Victoria's rule; in France, the rural/urban shift was less marked, but faith in "la Patrie" and its dominions prevailed; in Russia, a vain attempt to maintain an essentially feudal system alongside the new industrialist/capitalist status quo was inevitably fated; but in Germany, a new nation without a resonant history, the world and its future might be rewritten.

Thus, imperialism, industrialization and changing social demographics came together during the 19th century to create a seismic shift in the way people, nations and states saw themselves. And one major product of this was aggressive ambition, expressed at the highest level. Germany's aspirations first found voice in the Franco-Prussian war of 1871-72 when, in an ambitious gambit to lay hold of the rich coal and ore fields of the Saar and Alsace-Lorraine, she delivered her armies to Paris. This fundamental threat to the European "system", effectively held in place since the defeat of Napoleon and the Congress of Vienna in 1815, got tails twitching and sabres rattling. International confrontations bubbled increasingly to the surface.

THE OPPOSING POWERS

KEY

- ALLIES: AUGUST 1914
- CENTRAL POWERS: AUGUST 1914
- NEUTRAL BUT SUBSEQUENTLY JOINED ALLIES, WITH DATE
- NEUTRAL BUT SUBSEQUENTLY JOINED CENTRAL POWERS, WITH DATE
- NEUTRAL THROUGHOUT THE WAR

SWEDEN

DENMARK

NORTH SEA

BALTIC SEA

GREAT BRITAIN

RUSSIAN EMPIRE

NETH.

GERMANY

BELGIUM

LUX

FRANCE

SWITZ.

AUSTRIA-HUNGARY

ATLANTIC OCEAN

ITALY
1915

ROMANIA
1916

SERBIA

BLACK SEA

PORTUGAL
1916

MONTENEGRO

BULGARIA
1915

SPAIN

ALBANIA

GREECE
1917

OTTOMAN EMPIRE
OCTOBER 1914

MEDITERRANEAN SEA

Archduke Frank Ferdinand and wife leaving the City Hall in Sarajevo 28th June 1914, shortly before being assassinated.

Punch magazine reflected German aggression in the 12 August 1914 issue.

Statistics tell their own tale. Between 1870 and 1914 the German population had doubled to around 65 million (Britain and France were around 40 million). By 1914, Germany's army, at 95 divisions, was twice the size of the French army, and twelve times larger than Britain's, while her navy, including some 20 modern battleships, easily outnumbered the French force and was able to rival the Royal Navy.

At the end of the 19th century, a series of political alliances were set up in an attempt to contain the situation. Germany forged an alliance based on common interest with Austria-Hungary in 1879, following it up with a pact with Russia – the "Three Emperors Alliance" in 1881. As Ottoman control of the Balkans was eroded, Austria concluded defensive alliances with Serbia and Romania, and Russia with Bulgaria, whilst France entered into an uneasy alliance with Russia to contain Germany in 1894, and extended the ironically-named "Entente Cordiale" to its old enemy Britain, in 1904, which was consolidated in 1908 in the Triple Alliance.

The assassination of the Austrian crown prince, Archduke Franz Ferdinand, and his wife, on a state visit to Sarajevo in June 1914 provided the short fuse which exploded into war. Austria delivered an ultimatum to Serbia for impossible and immediate reparations, and when these were (as expected) rejected, she declared war. The alliance system swung into operation: Russia unexpectedly ordered general mobilization; Germany sent an ultimatum to the tsar concerning the massing of troops along her eastern borders, and when this was ignored, declared war on Russia on 1 August.

However, in order to be able to counter the massive threat posed by Russia, Germany decided to deal with what was perceived as a lesser problem first: relying on a long-standing scheme, Germany implemented the Schlieffen Plan, designed to knock out the Low Countries and neutralize France by seizing Paris. On 3 August, Germany declared war on France, and the following day invaded Belgium, the first manoeuvre on their march to France. Britain promptly declared war on Germany, and Austria declared war on Russia. The Great War had begun.

The Germans enter Brussels August 1914. The Belgian Army retreated to Antwerp, but maintained continued resistance.

One of the modern armoured cupola positions at Maubeuge, which proved an unexpected obstavcle for the advancing Germans.

By August 1914, Europe was already divided into two opposing groups of countries, but upon the outbreak of war, each side sought more allies. The Ottoman Empire joined the Central Powers, Germany and Austria-Hungary, in October, and Bulgaria joined them in 1915. The Entente (or Allied) powers of France, Russia and Great Britain were joined perforce by Belgium, and by Italy (1915), Portugal and Romania (1916) and Greece in 1917, while Britain persuaded the non-European powers of Japan and the USA to eventually support the Allied cause, turning a European war into a World war.

The Belgian Army put up a stiff but ultimately doomed resistance to the might of the German military machine, but bought the French Army time to assemble a mass defense of the Franco-Belgian frontier, while the British Expeditionary Force was sent across the Channel to bolster the French left flank in Flanders. Nevertheless, by 26 August the so-called 'Battle of the Frontiers' had proved incapable of stemming the German tide, and the French fell back to new defensive positions south of the River Marne. Only here, after a desperate struggle, would the Germans be brought to a standstill in early September.

The Germans were facing additional problems. The Russians had crossed Germany's eastern borders on 17 August, and Germany called on Austria to help staunch the wound. A massive clash occurred at Tannenburg, involving the first of the astronomical casualty figures which were to mark the course of the war: 50,000 Russians were killed and 100,000 Russian prisoners taken. Three Russian corps had been destroyed, and a further two put to flight. In many ways this battle of encirclement proved Germany's outstanding military success during the war, as on the Western Front any progress was grinding to a halt.

The British Infantry enter Ypres Oct 1914. The British were to take over various sections of the front in Flanders; the battle at Ypres between 19 October and 22 November was their most notable and testing victory in 1914.

'We were lined up and given a very generous issue of rum. I didn't even drink beer. So in no time we were quite euphoric really. We were quite happy. We didn't know where we were going, but the moon broke through the clouds and it was a lovely night. And I can remember, as we marched along, we passed a Roman Catholic priest who removed his hat and murmured his blessings.'

Private Clifford Lane, 1st Battalion, Hertfordshire Regiment

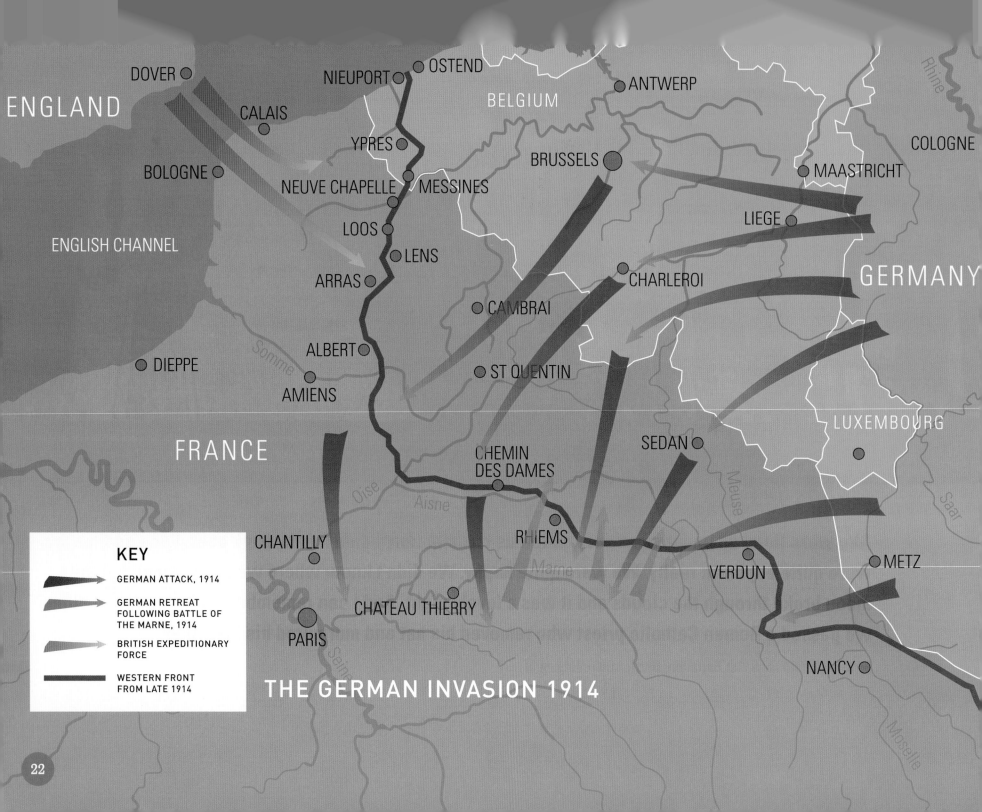

ENGLAND

DOVER

CALAIS

BOLOGNE

ENGLISH CHANNEL

DIEPPE

FRANCE

NIEUPORT

OSTEND

BELGIUM

ANTWERP

COLOGNE

MAASTRICHT

YPRES

BRUSSELS

NEUVE CHAPELLE

MESSINES

LIEGE

LOOS

CHARLEROI

GERMANY

LENS

ARRAS

CAMBRAI

ALBERT

ST QUENTIN

AMIENS

Somme

LUXEMBOURG

CHEMIN
DES DAMES

SEDAN

Oise

Aisne

Meuse

Saar

CHANTILLY

RHIEMS

Marne

METZ

VERDUN

KEY

GERMAN ATTACK, 1914

GERMAN RETREAT
FOLLOWING BATTLE OF
THE MARNE, 1914

BRITISH EXPEDITIONARY
FORCE

WESTERN FRONT
FROM LATE 1914

CHATEAU THIERRY

Seine

PARIS

NANCY

Rhine

Moselle

THE GERMAN INVASION 1914

The northernmost extent of the Western Front
trench systems on the Belgian coast.

The southernmost extent at the Swiss Alps

But apart from now conducting a war on two fronts, supplies of munitions were running low, and distance and supply logistics were thwarting Germany's ability to press its armies forward. Following French Commander-in-Chief Joffre's tactical success in holding the Marne front north of Paris, there now ensued a 'race to the sea' as the Germans sought to sweep around the French left flank, but each initiative was countered by French, retreating Belgian, and British forces. Eventually, in October the front line met the North Sea on the Belgian coast between Nieuport and Ostend.

As Winter set in, and the armies dug in, the positions ossified into a continuous line running for over 450 miles from the North Sea to the Swiss border - the Western Front had been born. What had been widely anticipated as a rapidly settled conflict was becoming a war of attrition on an industrial scale.

'The winter of '14 was extremely hard because we had no amenities whatsoever. It was just ditches, the trenches were just waterlogged ditches, and one was often up to one's knees in frozen mud. You could do nothing about it except stick there.'

Private Reginald Haine, 1st Battalion, Honourable Artillery Company

French infantry – *poilous* – being enthusiastically waved off to war by a crowd in 1914. Issues such as height and weight were rapidly set aside as the need to rapidly build the army rapidly became clear. France also drew in troops from its African colonies almost immediately.

German troops leave for the front, August 1914. The railway system was essential to the German Army's mobility and its ability to deploy or reposition troops.

To fuel this full-scale war, huge conscript armies began to be mobilized across Europe. Those countries with overseas interests also sought the involvement of the subjects of their colonies, ensuring the conflict became a truly global affair.

Relative army sizes differed considerably, however. In peace time, for example, the German Army had numbered 840,000 troops, which was transformed very quickly by conscription to more than 4,000,000 when war was declared. The French were able to muster 3,500,000 troops through conscription, although by 1915 half a million had been sent back to work in the factories that were placed under military control.

The British Army numbered only 750,000 in total. Lord Kitchener, the newly- appointed Secretary for State for War in Britain, mindful of the relatively small size of the army at his disposal, and not convinced that this would be a short war, mounted a hugely successful campaign to recruit volunteers to fight, 'Your Country Needs You'.

Recruiting stations the length and breadth of Great Britain were besieged by young men wanting to 'sign up'.

French uniform (left), German uniform (right),1914

Kitchener's enormously successful recruitment poster. It was this initiative that led to the 'New Army', many of whom were to see action for the first time on the Somme in 1916.

Seemingly endless queues formed outside recruiting offices, as here in Whitehall, London.

By the time conscription in Britain was eventually introduced in May 1916, the total of volunteers had grown to 2,600,000. As in France, this left the factories and offices depleted. The introduction in 1914 of the Defence of the Realm Act (DORA) gave the British government powers to direct industry, the economy and aspects of public life (the introduction of licensing hours for public houses for example).

In fact, the issue of supply and munitions proved critical on all fronts very rapidly. The Prussian War Ministry was to virtually run out of shells within six weeks, a problem also faced by the French. Both Russia and the Central Powers realized that they would need the support of a healthy civilian population to sustain their war efforts. And both France and Britain were soon to address how best they could disrupt the supply of food and other essentials to the populations of their adversaries.

'...one feels that little shiver run up the back, and you know you have got to do something. I had just turned 17 at the time, and I went up to Whitehall and enlisted'

Private William Dove, 16th Lancers

Neatly suited young recruits holding the Bible and taking the oath of allegiance..

A recruit takes an eyesight test.

A variety of reasons no doubt induced British men to volunteer that summer. There were a number of industrial disputes threatening economic stability, and a fresh crop of school leavers keen to make their mark in the world. Being accused of cowardice too, was a fear.

With the stories of their father's heroism ringing in their ears about the Boer War, many young men were anxious to do their bit for King and Country too. The legacy of Victorian imperialism, and the benefits it had brought the Old Country were not in question, and patriotism ran high. Further, for many years anti-German propaganda had fuelled the popular belief that 'the Hun' needed sorting out.

Having signed up they had to swear an oath of allegiance and undertake a medical to be pronounced fit. For many men this must have seemed like a great adventure – the opportunity to wear a uniform, earn money and travel abroad – hopefully returning by Christmas, when they were assured it would be all over.

The new volunteer army would need training and equipping – no small matter – but also given more motivation than just enthusiasm. General Sir Henry Rawlinson shared his view with Lord Derby that men would be more likely to fight effectively as a unit if they fought alongside their friends and colleagues.

Derby promoted the idea, and the first 'Pals' battalion was formed – the 'Liverpool Pals', an idea which gained immediate popularity, spreading rapidly across Northern England. Workforces from factories and collieries joined up en masse, and soon the idea was attracting clerks, accountants indeed groups of men from all walks of life across the nation.

British uniform, 1914

The Grimsby Chums, 10th Battalion, Lincolnshire Regiment, on initial firearms training. Early in the war there were enough arms available for training, but this was soon to become a problem. Note that uniforms have not yet been issued

'I was walking down Camden High Street when two young ladies approached and said: "Why aren't you in the Army with the boys?" So I said, "I'm sorry, I'm only seventeen" and one of them said "Oh, we've heard that one before"...Then she put her hand in her bag and pulled out a feather"

Private SC Lang

The Royal Scots Fusiliers dig in at Ypres October 1914. The lines often followed existing road patterns, the removed earth being thrown up in front of the trench to provide a rampart.

The relative stalemate that now prevailed by late Autumn 1914 led both sides to consolidate their position, by 'digging in'.

This meant the construction of a series of complex trenches and secure dugouts. The opposing trenches varied considerably in terms of design and construction, the German ones by far superior to the British and French ones. The Germans anticipated a long, drawn-out war, and expended considerable effort in contructing deep concrete bunkers designed to withstand shelling, with well- equipped accomodation for the troops. The Allies however, assumed that their trenches would be for the winter season at best

and therefore put less effort into their construction, the more permanent ones being lined with wattles, planking or sandbags. The trenches were surmounted by swathes of impregnable barbed wire. This new, static trench warfare gave rise to the development of specific weapons to be used for launching short-range attacks and regular trench raids (usually conducted at night) such as trench mortars and grenades, periscopes for observation, rifles fitted with wire cutters, and brutal trench clubs.

As the troops settled into their positions over the Winter 1914-15 so the trench systems grew, with various communication trenches and successive lines

German trench mortar

Royal Scots Fusiliers at Neuve Chapelle, south of Ypres, Winter 1914-15. Trench life in the Winter months combined bitter cold, often resulting in frostbite with frequent flooding of the trenches, leading to the widespread condition of 'trenchfoot', insanitary latrines, and widespread boredom. In the Summer months, lice became a major problem.

being constructed to enable troops to move up to the front, and withdraw, sheltered in part from sniper, machine-gun and artillery fire. The rear trenches were enlarged to accommodate small artillery pieces such as the German *minenwerfer* trench mortar.

'...we made these hand grenades out of jam-tin bombs and just hurled then into the German trenches. They were very successful.'

Captain Reginald Thomas, Royal Artillery

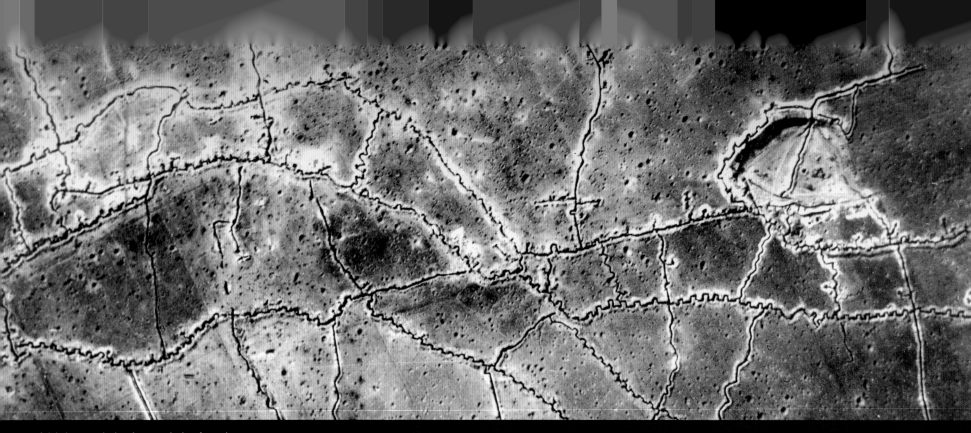

Ariel photograph showing complexity of trench systems.

German trench systems were positioned to take advantage of tactical factors such as terrain, defensibility, elevation and potential fields of fire – the French coalfields would be defended vigorously but the location of the German positions along the Western Front was not always the result of such considerations. Meanwhile, the stabilization of the Western Front allowed the Germans to concentrate greater military effort against the Russians on the Eastern Front.

However during April and May of 1915, the Germans did launch an offensive in the Ypres area that was notable for the first major use of gas. The Allies,

fearful of the potentially devastating effects of this new weapon had to mass manufacture gas masks as a priority.

Other new technologies rapidly made their appearance on the front, including radio telecommunications and airplanes. Telephones and wireless became intrinsic aspects of communications, and operating across such a large front, soon became essential. However, wireless sets were on the whole cumbersome and delicate to be of much practical use under shellfire, and telephone wires and cables were often destroyed. The most effective way of means of communication proved to be the most basic: carrier pigeons, dogs and runners.

Field 'wireless' set, able to receive Morse code

Argyle and Southern Highlanders wearing pad respiratory gas protection, June 1915.

A line of single-seater Sopwith Camel fighter planes of the Royal Flying Corps.

German gas mask

Aircraft were initially used for aerial reconnaissance and reconnaissance photography; in 1915 they began to be adapted to carry bombs and had machine guns fitted, while purpose built bombers and fighters were being put into production on all home fronts. None of these had great range, and were used largely for tactical support.

January 1915 saw the Germans unleash another secret weapon when a Zeppelin airship raided Great Yarmouth. In May, London became the first city undergo a sustained strategic bombing attack. The war was now being brought from the front line to the civilians at home.

At sea, by April 1915 the Royal Navy had achieved supremacy, and had begun a blockade of the North Sea in an attempt to starve Germany. The German response involved another new weapon – an unrestricted U-Boat campaign began in February against Allied shipping.

While the war widened beyond the battlefields of the Western Front, the armies there began to gather their strengths for what were envisaged on both sides to be war-winning, breakthrough offensives planned for the following year. The Germans showed their hand first with a concentrated assault on Verdun. 1916 would prove to be the crucible of the Great War.

THE GERMAN DEFENCES ON THE SOMME

When the Western Front had been sketched in during the early months of the War, the Germans had arraigned themselves quite handsomely on the Somme. They had tried to ensure that before giving up any ground, they would have a ready-to-occupy defence sited further back in a more advantageous position. They would then withdraw back to this, leaving their opponents with an even harder task of moving them. Across the entire British attack front of 1 July, the German defenders had chosen their ground very carefully, taking maximum advantage of the terrain and in many places having clear views of the British trenches.

On the Somme they had had almost eighteen months to dig themselves in and their front line consisted of not just a single trench, but a three-line trench system. Each trench in the 'Front line' was about 200 yards apart and stitched together with an efficient network of communication trenches. At certain points, key strategic fortresses hardened this line, such as the Schwaben and Hawthorn redoubts. Often, French villages they had taken over were incorporated into this deep and solid defensive line, with the houses – and particularly the cellars – being reinforced by concrete. Deep, reinforced shelters with multiple exits were a feature all along the German Somme emplacements, and were large enough to accommodate the entire trench garrison. And, in front of the first trench, would be sited thick tangled belts of barbed wire, normally around thirty yards wide.

Around 2000 yards behind all this would then stand the German Second Position. On the Somme, this sector ran down the Thiepval Ridge to Pozières and on through Guillemont. This Second Position had very similar defensive characteristics to their Front line. 3000 yards behind this, they made progress in the construction of yet a Third Position. Much of this work was done by prisoners of war from the Eastern Front.

It has often been remarked that the German trenches were of a higher standard than either the British or French, but the obvious reason for this is that the Germans assumed that they were there for the duration. The British and French, on the other hand, saw their trenches purely as temporary devices, to be left behind when they had driven the Germans back.

Main Picture:
German machine-gun crew.
1. Captured German underground shelter at Bernafay Wood, Montauban, 3rd July.
2. German howitzer.

General Sir Douglas Haig. Part of the Scottish whisky distilling family, Haig was also a devout member of the Church of Scotland, and fully believed that God was on his side. Arguably, Haig was the most controversial character of the war. He was 55 when he came to the post of Commander-in-Chief of the British Army in France and Belgium. Strangely, he was not immediately given the rank of field-marshal, remaining a general, the same rank as his subordinate commanders.

On 19 December 1915 General Sir Douglas Haig was appointed Commander-in-Chief of the British Expeditionary Force, taking over from Sir John French, who it was felt had "underperformed" at both Neuve Chapelle and Loos. One of Haig's first official duties was attendance ten days later at a major conference of all the Allies, including Russia, in the French town of Chantilly. It was hosted by the French, and Joffre, as the overall Commander of the Allies, set the agenda. There was general agreement that in the coming year the Allies should open offensives against the Germans on both the Eastern and Western Fronts. France was locked into a life or death struggle with Germany, focussed on the fortress city of Verdun but Joffre was not sure the British were as committed. He needed the British to be fighting on the same terms, and politically he saw that a joint Franco-British attack, with both countries' armies fighting side by side, would ensure this. The junction of the two armies was in the Département of the Somme. To Joffre's mind this was the place to fight a mutual offensive and he demanded a 60 mile-long front be opened along this junction of the two armies. This major offensive would hit the Germans with the combined strength of 39 French and 25 British divisions.

THE CONFERENCE AT CHANTILLY

29 DECEMBER 1915

Haig did not see any strategic advantage to this plan at all, and considered the Somme a completely inappropriate location to attack. They all knew the Germans had constructed extremely strong defences there, taking every advantage of the rolling terrain of the countryside in the siting of their positions, and, moreover, Haig's preference for Flanders (to the west) was strategically far more effective, with major cities and railheads under German occupation, not to mention U-Boat pens sitting off the Belgian coast. The British could see no reason at all to fight the Germans on the Somme. However, they were the junior partners in the alliance, and Haig had no alternative but to defer to Joffre's demands. Haig and the British delegation left Chantilly deeply dissatisfied. They had been forced to commit their nation's troops to a huge attack whose motives were to them other than strategic. Chantilly was the genesis of the slaughter on the Somme.

General Joseph Joffre, the Allied Commander-in-Chief. He was anxious to have his British allies fighting on the same terms as France – in a life or death struggle with Germany (France had already lost a substantial percentage of their eventual total war dead). He thought that a joint offensive – at his place of choosing – was the way to achieve this. It was Joffre who demanded that the Somme be this place.

"ILS NE PASSERENT PAS"

The French rallying call.

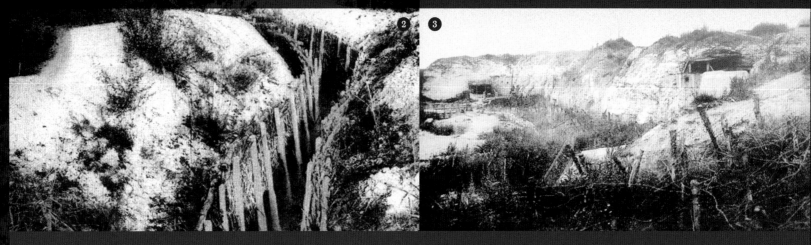

1, 2, 3. The fortifications at Fort Douamont, the French military stronghold at Verdun, a hundred miles east of Paris.

VERDUN

On 21 February 1916 the Germans launched a massive, all-out assault on the French fortress city of Verdun. This was to become a grinding, attritional battle that would drag on for the rest of the year, sucking in ever increasing numbers of French troops and materiel. The French had already sustained huge losses in the war, and the German plan was to continue this process in order to "bleed the French white". Psychologically, the fall of Verdun, a strong military base just a hundred miles east of Paris, would have seriously undermined the morale of the French nation. They were determined to hold it at all costs and practically every French division took its turn in the cauldron of Verdun. On the German side, their losses at Verdun (some 370,000) were to be dwarfed by their casualties on the Somme, which exceeded 600,000.

The battle at Verdun also held ominous significance for the British. The abstract plans for an offensive on the Somme that were made at Chantilly in December at once assumed an urgent dimension, with the French demanding that it start as soon as possible, to divert German troops away from Verdun. It also meant the British now playing the greater part in the attack: they immediately took over more of the French sector, releasing French troops to reinforce at Verdun, and Haig assumed command of the joint armies on the Somme. Joffre's original demand for a 60 mile-long front was consequently scaled down to around half that.

Together with his generals, Haig set in train the mammoth logistical planning for an attack in August but, by May, the French situation at Verdun had considerably worsened and there were repeated appeals to the British to "do something" – culminating in a bad-tempered meeting between the commanders. Haig climbed down and the Somme attack was brought forward to July, although yet a further meeting ensued, with Joffre bringing along General Foche, the French President and Prime Minister to further twist Haig's arm. He was forced to give way again and the attack on the Somme was finally agreed for late June 1916.

A German sniper at Verdun. The remains of a French *poilou* lies half-buried by his side.
Right: Three present-day views of Fort Douamont. After the war, what remained from the battle for Verdun was designated a French national memorial.

The detailed level of planning by the British for the Somme offensive was the most complex logistical operation they had ever undertaken and should have assured victory. There were, however, no contingency plans should any aspect of the attack fail.

❶ ❷

Green Line, or
Fourth Army Objectives for
1ST July (1ST July)

French Objective for 1ST July

Army Boundary

SCALE

MILE 1 ½ 0   1   2   3   4   5 MILES

Heights in metres

3100/31.

Ordnance Survey 1929.

THE PLAN

1. The British line from Serre down to Montauban and the junction with the French Sixth Army, around 1 July. The map also shows the British and French objectives as dotted lines.
2. Soldiers of the East Yorks making their way up to the line near Serre in the days leading up to the 1st July.

Verdun fundamentally altered Haig's vision of the year's campaign. He had brought to his role a burning desire to beat the German Army in 1916, but after the attack on Verdun he was forced to modify his objectives. His task now was to help stave off a French defeat at Verdun, to inflict 'grievous losses' on the Germans, and to put the Allies into a war-winning situation the following year, 1917. In January he had reorganized his armies, and the newly-formed Fourth Army, under the command of General Sir Henry Rawlinson, was to bear the brunt of the summer attack.

One of Haig's main concerns was the inexperience of his New Army troops and for weeks, the British High Command pored over their maps and papers, shuffling around the different parts of the divisions, brigades, even battalions, in an attempt to evolve a battle-winning strategy. Almost every Regular and Territorial Army division was given a quota of the volunteers, whilst the New Army divisions were 'stiffened' by an injection of experienced men.

Although Haig was the Commander-in-Chief, Rawlinson held the same rank and was almost the same age. Consequently, the relationship was almost one of parity. Rawlinson held great sway – after all, it was Haig who had appointed him. The Somme was to be his battle. He submitted his plan of attack to Haig and stubbornly held out for most of it, despite Haig's

concerns. Rawlinson had noted how the Germans had begun their attack at Verdun by completely destroying the French front line trenches with a tremendous bombardment. The German infantry had then poured in. He intended to employ precisely this tactic on the Somme. With his great faith in his artillery, he advocated the heaviest bombardment yet seen in the War, after which his troops had merely to occupy the destroyed defences. The troops to were to steadily walk over to the shattered German defences – an idea completely at odds with prevailing assault tactics.

Rawlinson's plan was then to hold this new front line against German counter-attacks from their Second Position and consolidate his gains, but Haig, anxious to get his cavalry into the action, wanted the troops to take both the First and Second German positions, thereby opening up the way for a cavalry breakthough.

Between them, the two generals agreed a compromise that left them both culpable: Rawlinson, for his part, knew that taking only the First German Position was the thing to do; on the other hand Haig also knew that by not rushing the enemy's trenches the assault troops would be dangerously exposed. Rawlinson was adamant – nothing would be left alive after his bombardment, and besides, his troops were insufficiently trained to adopt more sophisticated tactics. But Haig was also adamant – he wanted both German lines taken in the same day. ▶▶

PLAN OF THE ATTACK 1 JULY 1916

KEY
- ALLIED FRONT LINE
- GERMAN FRONT LINE
- GERMAN SECOND POSITION
- GERMAN THIRD POSITION
- DIVISIONAL BOUNDARY
- BRITISH ATTACK
- FRENCH ATTACK
- MINE CRATER
- TOWN/VILLAGE
- REDOUBT
- WOOD
- ROAD
- RAILWAY

BRITISH THIRD ARMY

46TH (N. MIDLAND) DIVISION

DIVERSIONARY ATTACK

GOMMECOURT
The Kaiser's Oak

56TH (LONDON) DIVISION

48TH (S. MIDLAND) DIVISION

(NO ATTACK HERE)

31ST DIVISION

SERRE
Redan Ridge
Heiden Kopf

4TH DIVISION

AUCHONVILLERS

BEAUMONT HAMEL

29TH DIVISION

SCHWABEN REDOUBT

36TH (ULSTER) DIVISION

49TH (WEST RIDING) DIVISION (IN RESERVE)

THIEPVAL WOOD
THIEPVAL
MOUQUET FARM

32ND DIVISION

Wonder Werk
Leipzig Salient
AVELUY WOOD
Nab (Blighty) Valley
Nord Werk

AUTHUILLE
AUTHUILLE WOOD

POZIÈRES

OVILLERS

8TH DIVISION
Mash Valley

BRITISH FOURTH ARMY

LA BOISSELLE
Usna Hill
Tara Hill

19TH (WESTERN) DIVISION (IN RESERVE)

34TH DIVISION

Sausage Valley

ALBERT

21ST DIVISION

FRICOURT

17TH (NORTHERN) DIVISION (IN RESERVE)

50TH BRIGADE OF 17TH (NORTHERN) DIVISION

MAMETZ

7TH DIVISION

9TH (SCOTTISH) DIVISION (IN RESERVE)

18TH (EASTERN) DIVISION

30TH DIVISION

FRENCH SIXTH ARMY

River Ancre

GERMAN FIRST ARMY FROM SEPTEMBER

BAPAUME

GERMAN XIV RESERVE CORPS

BUTTE DE WARLENCOURT

HIGH WOOD

GERMAN SECOND ARMY

BAZENTIN LE PETIT
BAZENTIN LE PETIT WOOD
BAZENTIN LE GRAND WOOD
BAZENTIN LE GRAND

DELVILLE WOOD
GINCHY

MAMETZ WOOD

TRONES WOOD
GUILLEMONT
LEUZE WOOD

MONTAUBAN
BERNAFAY WOOD

GERMAN SECOND ARMY FROM SEPTEMBER

0   1
Mile

And so the plan emerged. An unprecedented bombardment would destroy the Germans' defences. The Fourth Army was then to take the German front line from Serre in the north of the attack, down to Montauban in the south, then onwards to take the German Second Position along Thiepval Ridge down to Guillemont. The French, meanwhile, were to take the German Front line astride the River Somme and advance towards the German Second Line at Maurepas down to Flaucourt, opposite Peronne. A diversionary attack was to be also to be launched at the same time by Allenby's Third Army at Gommecourt, two miles north of Serre, but there would be no attack at all between the two locations.

The build-up of materiel for the offensive was on an awesome scale, and had to be assembled as near the front as possible. Horses, shells, trench mortars were shipped across in their thousands, notwithstanding the massive quantities of food and fodder and the logistics of water supply, which involved sinking wells and laying miles of pipe.

PREPARING FOR THE 'BIG PUSH'

General preparations showing various aspects of the build-up: the British Army brought over to France more than 60,000 horses; endless columns of lorries brought thousands of cases of shells up to the line. The devices shown above are trench mortars. They were known as "plum puddings" and were bright orange in colour. It was only discovered after 1 July that many of these had failed to detonate. As all these supplies were being brought in, divisions and divisions of troops were being marched up to the front.

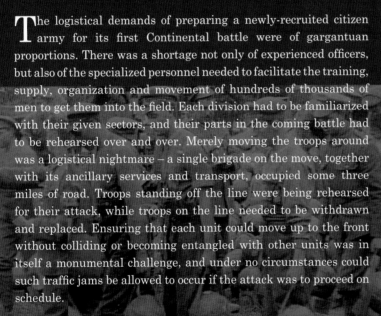

The logistical demands of preparing a newly-recruited citizen army for its first Continental battle were of gargantuan proportions. There was a shortage not only of experienced officers, but also of the specialized personnel needed to facilitate the training, supply, organization and movement of hundreds of thousands of men to get them into the field. Each division had to be familiarized with their given sectors, and their parts in the coming battle had to be rehearsed over and over. Merely moving the troops around was a logistical nightmare – a single brigade on the move, together with its ancillary services and transport, occupied some three miles of road. Troops standing off the line were being rehearsed for their attack, while troops on the line needed to be withdrawn and replaced. Ensuring that each unit could move up to the front without colliding or becoming entangled with other units was in itself a monumental challenge, and under no circumstances could such traffic jams be allowed to occur if the attack was to proceed on schedule.

In the months leading up to the battle, massive improvements also had to be made to the roads and railways in this quite isolated, rural part of France. Supplying this number of men with the minimum basic of fresh water alone took enormous organization to put in place.

Communications, the lifeline between the Front line and Command, was one more vital piece of the system – five hundred miles of cable had been laid, some at a depth of six feet, for every mile of front in the forward areas. To the rear of Divisional Headquarters, 3000 miles of wire linked the forward areas, through every stage of liaison and command, right back to General Sir Douglas Haig himself.

As the preliminary bombardment drew near, the many hundreds of howitzers and big guns were brought in, and endless columns of lorries carried vast quantities of shells, supplies and all the paraphernalia of war up to the forward areas. Putting in place its supply chain and gearing up for an offensive of this scale was a completely new experience for the British and, as was to be discovered in the aftermath of the First Day, vital components in this chain were to prove seriously defective.

By the early summer, not so much an army, but 'a complex society' had been engendered in northern France. The British troops massing around the Somme took very easily to the local countryside. It reminded many of them of home. It had not yet been destroyed by shellfire. The early summer weather helped. Trees were blossoming, and many noted peaceful birdsong. Men bathed and fished in the streams. For many, of course, it was their first time away from home – certainly abroad. It all felt like a big holiday adventure, a bit of a "lark". The 13th Battalion of The Rifle Brigade at Auxi-le-Château contained many sportsmen, and amongst the Olympic athletes and rugby players, seventeen golf professionals had all joined up together. For The Golfers, as they were known, the gentle slopes of the area were reminders of the famous courses they knew back in Blighty. Many of the officers were glad to join them on their improvised greens to brush up their technique under professional tutelage.

45

The empty shell cases piled up – over a million shells were fired during the seven-day bombardment.

THE BOMBARDMENT

During the first three weeks of June the guns had been brought up at night and stealthily put into position. After settling the guns in, the artillerymen carefully registered all their targets, with the aid of forward observation officers, balloons and aeroplanes. Then they waited. The bombardment got under way on 24 June 1916. It was Midsummer's Day. It was planned to last five days, with the attack starting on 29 June.

There were to be twice as many guns ranged across the British attack front compared with the battle at Loos, and there was an artillery piece for every seventeen yards of the German Front to be attacked. The artillerymen had a daily routine of firing an 80-minute concentrated barrage, using all the guns. After which, a steadier, but continuous firing continued for the remainder of the day. At night, half the guns were rested, but the fire was made up with machine-guns putting down an harassing fire to the rear of the front line, to disrupt the defenders supplies and relief columns. At night the scene

was spectacular, and one hundred miles away, in Kent and along the southern coast of England, it could plainly be heard. Tell-tale signs, such as munitions workers having to work through their May Bank Holiday period, allowed many people in England to suspect that the 'Big Push' was imminent.

Despite the powerful display, there was a crucial shortage of heavy guns that were necessary to destroy the deeper German dugouts – indeed half of those the British were using had been loaned from the French. Another key aspect of the bombardment too was to destroy the German barbed wire, allowing the attacking troops into the German trenches. This was to be done by the 18lb guns firing shrapnel shells. These demanded a high degree of accuracy from the gunner when setting his fuses. Too soon and the shells exploded in the air. Too late, and they exploded in the ground. A fine art that too often failed.

A heavy rail gun in action during the bombardment.

'My God! When we go across to Thiepval, all we'll find is the caretaker and his dog!'

Major-General WH Rycroft, Commanding Officer, 32nd Division

As well as the continuous bombardment, the British increased the number of trench raids, in an effort to ascertain the effectiveness of the shelling. Reports varied, and some officers and infantry began to raise concerns – many officers could plainly see through their field glasses that much of the wire was still intact. Rawlinson's confident assertions that 'nothing would exist at the conclusion of the bombardment' were beginning to be doubted. Other doubts were surfacing too. At the same time as the bombardment was beginning, the Somme weather took a hand in the build-up. Two violent thunderstorms, on the 23rd and the 26th June, were accompanied by heavy rain, which continued on and off until the 28th – ostensibly the evening before the attack, but by then Zero Hour had been postponed for 48 hours, to 1 July. By that time, 150,000 shells every day for a whole week had been fired, more than in the whole first twelve months of the War.

"One night on one of our trench raids I was captured. I was told to leave the dugout and run after the German in front of me whilst another followed behind. I was running for a long time and climbing over huge shells that had not exploded, I must have seen hundreds of them. Duds"

Private F McLaughlin, 1st Royal Dublin Fusiliers

47

THE EVENING BEFORE THE ATTACK

'As we staggered up to the trenches we passed our divisional commander with some of his staff. His words of cheer to us were, "Good luck, men. There is not a German left in their trenches, our guns have blown them all to Hell." Then, I suppose, he got into his car and went home to his HQ to wine and dine, while we poor benighted blighters tottered on our way to glory.'

Private AV Pearson, Leeds Pals

A divisional commander gives words of encouragement to some of his troops on the eve of the attack.

On 30 June, the attack troops stored away their personal effects, handed in their greatcoats, and prepared to begin the long march towards their appointment with destiny. The rain storms which had delayed the offensive were over and it had turned into a fine summer's afternoon. It was a deeply emotional time in the dozens of billeting villages behind the lines. Hardened regimental sergeant-majors had tears streaming down their cheeks as the men marched out. Many divisional and corps commanders turned out to assure their men of the already completed demoralization and destruction of the enemy. To the 11th Sherwood Foresters: 'You will meet nothing but dead Germans. You will advance to Mouquet Farm and be there by 11am. The field kitchens will follow you and give you a good meal.'

As they settled down to march the final kilometres up to the Front, some units sang to pass the time, but most fell to quiet contemplation of the events ahead. Men of the Sheffield City Battalion were concerned to see several German balloons, or "sausages" as they called them, flying overhead, plainly observing the many thousands of Tommies marching towards the line. The route of some attack troops took them past large, freshly dug pits – mass graves ready for burying the dead of tomorrow. ▶▶

1. Men of the 4th Battalion, Worcester Regiment ready to move up to the line. They have wire-cutters attached to their rifles.
2. Troops of the 2nd Royal Warwicks, 7th Division enjoying a last hot meal before moving up to their jumping-off trenches.

With such huge numbers of troops to get into position all along the attack front, the communication trenches were packed tightly with men shuffling backwards and forwards in a state of high anticipation and nervousness, trying to find their places. Coarse language was the order of the day. Some poor troops had been there two days already – when the attack had been postponed from 29th June there had been no logistical way of getting them out of the line, then back in. They'd had to endure two days in the cold and rain, but the waiting was almost over. It was only now that the troops were told the time of the attack. Many were shocked to realise that they would be going over in broad daylight, rather than the usual pre-dawn timing. Rum rations were given out, and some units allowed the men as much rum as they wanted. Some companies, where the captain was a strict teetotaller, got none at all.

The British barrage started up for one last time before Zero Hour, with increased intensity: '...it was now that the nervous tension pressed hardest upon them. Men knelt down and prayed – God seemed very near to them at this time; some took out their pay books and completed that page which contained a form for making out a will; others stared at photographs of their families which they kissed before returning to their pockets: 'I gave myself a sad thought of home. At this particular time it would be milking time. The cows would be coming in from the meadows and everything would be lovely and peaceful at my father's farm, in the little village at the foot of the Sperrin mountains.'
Pte L Bell, Derry Volunteers

**'With God's help I feel hopeful.
The men are in splendid spirits.'**
General Sir Douglas Haig, excerpt from his diary.

Geoffrey Malins in the field.

FILMING THE BATTLE

Geoffrey Malins was one of the British Army's earliest "Kinematographers". At the outbreak of war he was working for Gaumont Pictures, and after some early experiences in Belgium he got a name for himself as a war photographer. Determined to 'get some stuff' on the 'Big Push', he approached the War Office, who got him to the 29th Division on the Somme. He spent a week filming the bombardment, the preparations, the men coming up to the line.

Early on 1 July Malins was asked to film the Lancashire Fusiliers as they waited for Zero Hour in the Sunken Lane (out in No Man's Land, and reached by a small tunnel dug during the night). 'Men were passing ammunition from one to another in an endless chain and disappearing into the bowels of the earth...By the light of an electric torch stuck in the earth I was able to see the men. They were wet with perspiration, steaming, in fact, stripped to the waist...' At the exit of the tunnel he got forward, hugging the bank as close as possible: 'a false step would have exposed the position to the Bosche who might have enfiladed the whole road from the flank.'

Successive frames showing the Hawthorn Ridge explosion.

'A false step would have exposed the position to the Bosche who might have enfiladed the whole road from the flank.'
Geoffrey Malins *from* 'How I Filmed the War'

Men of the 1st Lancashire
Fusiliers waiting in the Sunken
Lane prior to going over at 7.30am

Making his way back, he was informed that a huge mine was to be exploded under the Hawthorn Redoubt, and he positioned himself with his lens pointing towards the site. At 7:19 he started turning the camera's handle, two revolutions per second. Time passed slowly, and he had exposed a lot of film. 'Would it go up before I had time to reload? The thought brought beads of perspiration to my forehead. The agony was awful, indescribable. My hand began to shake.' Then up it went, and he had to steady himself and the camera against the shaking of the ground and the repercussive effects of the explosion.

He continued turning, catching the Engineers leaping over the parapet with wire to secure the crater, then later on men retreating from the ridge after the failure of the assault at Beaumont Hamel. His edited film "The Battle of the Somme" was shown in picture houses throughout Great Britain. It has been estimated that at least half the population went to see it, with applause ringing round the auditoria at the appearance of the tanks!

53

'Suddenly, for a few seconds, all seemed silent, the barrage had quietened down. I walked up and down the footboards, saying to the men, "it's a walk-over." I had almost a feeling of disappointment. It was short-lived.'

Lieutenant M Asquith, 1st Barnsley Pals at Serre 1 July 1916

ZERO HOUR

Men of the 1st Lancashire Fusiliers going over at 7:30 on the morning of 1 July from King Street, part of the White City trench system at Beaumont Hamel. The still is from Geoffrey Malins' film of the battle.

46th (NORTH MIDLAND) DIVISION

THIRD ARMY - ALLENBY

● GOMMECOURT

□ The Kaiser's Oak

56th (LONDON) DIVISION

46th (North Midland) Division: Major-General Hon. EJ Montagu-Stuart-Wortley

56th (London) Division: Major-General CPA Hull

DIVERSION AT GOMMECOURT

'When we got to the German wire I was absolutely amazed to see it intact after what we had been told. The colonel and I took cover behind a small bank but after a bit the colonel raised himself to see better. Immediately, he was hit in the forehead by a single bullet.'

Private AH Tomlinson, Sherwood Foresters

1. The London Scottish marching up to the front.
2. The Official History map of the diversionary attack at Gommecourt, showing the trench lines and movements of individual units.

Whilst Rawlinson's Fourth Army mounted the 1 July offensive proper, a substantial diversionary attack took place at Gommecourt, site of a prominent German redoubt and also the most westerly point on the whole Western Front. It was conducted by two divisions of General Sir Edward Allenby's Third Army, the 46th (North Midland) Division and 56th (London) Division. The 46th North Midland Division was to attack around the north side of the woodland and meet up, at the rear of the village, with the 56th (London) Division, who were to attack from the south. This pincer movement was designed to cut off the garrison and break the German position.

At 7:20am both divisions released smokescreens and the troops lined up in No Man's Land under this cover. The London Division's first wave was relatively successful, with the German wire having been effectively cut. Queen Victoria's Rifles, the London Rifle Brigade, the Rangers and 1st London Scottish all accomplished their initial objective in taking the first two lines of German trenches. However, they gradually became detached from the following troops by an intense German counter-barrage on No Man's Land and their jumping off trenches. To the north, the covering smoke of the 46th North Midlanders was so thick at Zero Hour that many men lost their way. The German wire on their front was not well cut and they were met by a fierce resistance. Despite this, companies of Sherwood Foresters reached and entered the first German trenchline. But the following waves of men were then caught in savage artillery and machine-gun fire from the north and were unable to follow up the initial breakthrough. That afternoon, various plans were made to renew the attack, but all were aborted. Meanwhile, in the south, a company of Kensingtons had managed to reach their isolated forward troops, but they were the last reinforcements to arrive. By the early afternoon they were still holding their gains, but the second line soon fell back to the Germans. At dusk, the Londoners gave up the German first line and withdrew to their trenches, suffering heavy casualties in No Man's Land. Similarly, the surviving Sherwood Foresters made their way back under cover of darkness.

'Two years in the making, ten minutes in the destroying. That was our history.'
John Harris *from* 'The Covenant with Death'.

SERRE: THE DEATH OF INNOCENCE

 31st Division. Major-General R Wanless O'Gowan

The 31st Division at Serre was composed entirely of Northern Pals battalions, and was the quintessence of The Pals' ideal. The men defined themselves not as members of the Fourth Army, nor even of the 31st Division, but as being a 'Barnsley Pal', an 'Accrington Pal', or part of 'the Hull Mob'. They had tremendous loyalty to each other, principally because most had joined up together. T'owd Twelfth, the Division's pioneers, came mostly from Charlesworth Pit on the outskirts of Leeds. Whole shifts of men from the colliery had marched into Leeds to enlist. The composition of the Division at Serre reflected thousands of lives back in the working class districts of the North: Accrington, Barnsley, Bradford, Durham, Hull, Leeds and Sheffield. The Sheffield City Battalion were, for the most part, office and clerical workers, whilst the 1st and 2nd Barnsley Pals were drawn mainly from collieries around the town. The 'Hull Mob', 92nd Brigade, comprised four battalions, known to themselves as 'The Hull Commercials', 'The Hull Tradesmen', 'The Hull Sportsmen', and the fourth – because it comprised men who were none of the above – 'T'others'. ▶▶

Sheffield Memorial Park, site of the Accrington Pals and the Sheffield City Battalion's position opposite Serre.

Accrington 'Pals' joining up and parading in front of the cotton mills in 1914.

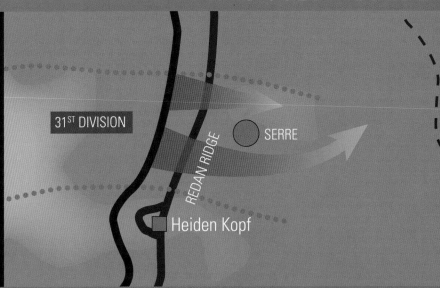

Over 2000 men were down within 30 minutes of going over the top.

Cartoon from *Punch* 25 November 1914.
Recruiting Officer: 'What regiment do you wish to join?'
Pitman: 'I don't care.'
Recruiting Officer: 'Sure you have no preference?'
Pitman: 'Well, put me in one o' them that spikes the beggars.'

On the evening of 30th June the four Hull battalions of 92 Brigade, which had been holding the Front line, withdrew, and the attack troops of 93 and 94 Brigade made the difficult seven-mile march across fields of mud into narrow, crowded trenches deep in water and semi-liquid mire, arriving between 2:00 and 4:00 in the morning – complete with their heavy kit loads. Despite this exhausting ordeal, they were in a state of expectation and excitement, heightened by the terrific bombardment still pounding the German front line. At 7:20am, as the hurricane barrage ended, companies of leading troops left the trenches, ran a hundred yards into No Man's Land and lay down. In turn, at 7:25am, the second half of the forward companies left the trench, dashed forward fifty yards and did likewise. At Zero Hour the whistles blew and out came the rest of the attacking troops. The forward troops in No Man's Land all stood up and together, at a steady walk, they headed for what they supposed was the cut German wire and their objectives beyond the front line.

The dreadful consequences of the flawed artillery barrage now came into play, for as the barrage stopped at 7:20 and lifted onto the German Second Positions further east, the Germans knew that now was the time for the front line troops to emerge from their protective shelters and defend their positions. Finally, after seven days of nightmarish shelling, the Tommies were coming. Out of the eerie quietness that had suddenly descended on the battlefield, men heard the sound of skylarks high above. Moments later came

a tremendous fire from the German side, both artillery and machine-guns. On the very left of the attack, savage machine gun fire from the north pushed the 2nd Barnsley Pals right – and directly into the path of the Sheffield City men. Soldiers from both battalions were mown down as they bunched together and searched vainly for gaps in the German wire. Eye-witness accounts say that some Sheffielders managed to evade the fire and enter the German front line. To their right, the Accrington Pals headed straight for the village but were very quickly devastated by sustained machine-gun fire. Similarly, on the extreme right of 31st's attack, the Leeds and Bradford men were also decimated – almost before they had left their trenches. Across the whole of No Man's Land and the British forward trenches the German artillery was firing a fierce and constant barrage. Later on, vague reports stated that a handful of Durhams had miraculously managed to get 2000 yards past the German front line into Pendant Copse, but then they had disappeared. They were never seen again.

Battalion commanders watched in horror as the carnage unfolded. Thirty minutes into the attack over 2000 men were down, either dead or wounded. By 10am, an officer sent forward to Nairne Trench on the left of the Division's attack could find nothing. The trench did not exist any more, and no trace of any survivors could be found either. On the steepest slope of the Divisional front, the British men had been wiped off the map.

REDAN RIDGE

'I could see that our leading waves had got caught by their kilts. They were killed hanging on the wire, riddled with bullets, like crows shot on a dyke.'

Private JS Reid, 2nd Seaforth Highlanders

4th Division. Major-General Hon. W Lambton

31ST DIVISION

SERRE

RIDGE

Heiden Kopf

REDAN

4TH DIVISION

AUCHONVILLERS

BEAUMONT HAMEL

HAWTHORN RIDGE

1. After the attack at Beaumont Hamel. A roll call for the 1st Lancashire Fusiliers in a reserve trench. The battalion had suffered 483 casualties.
2. Postcard of a German machine-gun crew. It was very often the strategically-placed machine-gun positions which caused much of the death and destruction on 1 July.

Redan Ridge is the featureless tract of upland that separates the villages of Serre and Beaumont Hamel. On the north of this ridge, just south-west of Serre, was the Heiden Kopf – the Quadrilateral Redoubt. In the direction towards Beaumont Hamel stood the Ridge Redoubt. It was 4th Division's task to take these two strongholds on their way to clearing the German lines east of Frankfurt Trench, which ran down the spine of the ridge. They would have a mere forty-five minutes to achieve this, before fighting their way into the German second line known as Munich Trench. The 4th was a Regular Army division, with survivors in its ranks from the original BEF – the 'Old Contemptibles' of 1914. However, its losses had been made good by drafts of Kitchener volunteers, so that for the most part its fighting soldiers had not yet seen action. It comprised battalions whose roots were in Ireland, Somerset, Scotland, Hampshire, Warwickshire, Essex and East Lancashire.

The attack on Redan Ridge was again a tragedy, although the assault had begun quite well at the Heiden Kopf. Two Birmingham battalions loaned to the 4th from 48th Division – the 6th and 8th Royal Warwicks – had stormed through the Redoubt and progressed almost 1000 yards into the German lines at Munich Trench. However, once there, they were met with strong resistance from a German force coming into the area. Further south, the situation was much the same as at Serre. The assaulting troops were subjected to heavy and sustained machine-gun fire before they had even left their jumping off trenches, not only from Ridge Redoubt, but also from Hawthorn Ridge, down at Beaumont Hamel. Only one small party of 1st East Lancs managed to reach the German Front line, and they were never heard from again.

Attending to the wounded at Beaumont Hamel.

29th Division. Major General Beauvoir de Lisle

BEAUMONT HAMEL

'We are now taking part in the greatest battle in which British troops have ever fought...You are not only fighting to maintain the honour of the 29th Division, which won its laurels on the Gallipoli Peninsula...You are fighting for your country. More than that, you are fighting for humanity.'

Major-General Beauvoir de Lisle, to his troops on the eve of the battle

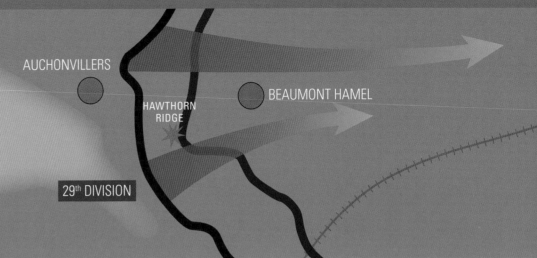

AUCHONVILLERS

HAWTHORN RIDGE

BEAUMONT HAMEL

29th DIVISION

A famous still from Malins' film showing the eruption of the mine placed underneath Hawthorn Ridge redoubt, at 7.20am. It contained 45,000lbs of high explosive.

Geographically, Beaumont Hamel was a difficult part of the line to patrol. It ran up and down various steep inclines whilst curving awkwardly from the White City trench system to the southern side of New Beaumont Road, where the land ran down to the River Ancre. When the 29th Division arrived in April 1916, they found the trenches to be in very poor condition and discovered also that the Germans were able to overlook many of the positions from the Schwaben Redoubt, on the far side of the Ancre valley. Consequently, the British Front here was susceptible to trench raids. The bulk of 29th Division at Beaumont Hamel was Regular Army, leavened by New Army volunteer units, notably the Public Schools Battalion, and the Newfoundland Regiment. 29th Division, including the 1st Lancashire Fusiliers, had already acquired a name for themselves in Gallipoli – 'The Incomparable' – and arrived ready to extend this reputation on the Somme.

Beaumont Hamel is one of the best remembered locations along the 1 July Front because Geoffrey Malins filmed here. Probably the two most widely-known shots are the Lancashire Fusiliers in The Sunken Lane, and the huge mine explosion at Hawthorn Ridge. The Hawthorn Ridge mine was detonated at 7:20am – a full ten minutes prior to Zero, thus alerting the Germans that the full attack was imminent. The British barrage was also ordered to lift away from the German front line at the same time. This gave the Germans, here at Beaumont Hamel, ample time to man their defences. And again, very few men ever reached the the German wire. All of the 29th suffered horrendous casualties, but it is worth mentioning the Newfoundland Regiment: their attack at 9:00am was made unsupported, and proved catastrophic – out of the 800 or so men and officers who attacked, at least 684 were killed, wounded, or disappeared. The Public Schools Battalion also suffered terrible casualties – 522 out of the attacking force of some 800 men.

65

SCHWABEN REDOUBT

36th (ULSTER) DIVISION

THIEPVAL WOOD

32ND DIVISION

THIEPVAL

THE ULSTERS AT THE SCHWABEN REDOUBT

36th (Ulster) Division. Major-General OSW Nugent

If the British could wrest control of the formidable Schwaben Redoubt, the Feste Schwaben, from the Germans, they would have the tactical key to unlock the whole of Thiepval Ridge. The high ground of Thiepval Ridge was an area of crucial importance to the Germans' defence of the Western Front in this sector. Since taking over the area around Thiepval in September 1914, they had built a labyrinth of trenches, deep bomb-proof shelters, control centres, and communications exchanges. From St. Pierre Divion down by the River Ancre, up to the steep slopes of the Feste Schwaben, a network of strongly-fortified positions had been constructed, with a series of connecting trenches back to their solid Second Position, which ran along Thiepval Ridge. It was the 36th (Ulster) Division's task to take this formidable front line position.

The 36th Ulsters were a New Army division, but with a twist. It was formed completely from the Protestant Ulster Defence Force (UDF), a private army controlled by several Ulster politicians led by Sir Edward Carson. It had over 80,000 members, all fully armed and already trained along military lines – ironically, its arms had been bought from Germany. Its purpose was to ensure a Protestant future for Ulster, and was willing to fight the British Government – or anyone else – to resist Home Rule by the majority Catholics. The Irish situation in 1914 was just as explosive as in more recent times.

1. The landscape at the Schwaben Redoubt and Thiepval.
2. Site of the 36th Ulsters' jumping-off trenches.
3. The corner of Thiepval Wood which formed the boundary of the 36th and 32nd Divisions.

'Come on boys, no surrender!'

Major George Gaffikin, West Belfast Battalion
(war cry from the battle of the Boyne)

By turns, Kitchener had persuaded Carson to encourage his men to volunteer, and now here they were on the Somme, in at the start of the 'Big Push'. Before Zero Hour the Ulsters crept out of their jumping-off trenches and laid up in No Man's land. Taking nothing for granted, they eschewed the idea of advancing at a steady pace, as per Fourth Army's orders, and at 7:30am they charged the German front line en masse. Such was their passion that they completely overran the German defenders. Legend has it that their success was down to a mix of Irish individualism, alcoholic bravura – and religious fervour. 1st July happened to fall on the anniversary of the Battle of the Boyne, and many of the men wore their Orange Order sashes into battle. In 'a glorious feat of arms' they poured through the front line and into the mighty defences of the Schwaben, taking 500 prisoners in the process. However, the failure of 29th Division's attack on their left and 32nd Division's attack to their right, left them overextended and completely without cover to their flanks.

By this time, German defenders in Thiepval Fort were able to turn their attention to the Ulsters. Subjected to fierce and extensive German counter-attacks from three sides, by the late afternoon the 36ths had suffered heavy casualties and were eventually forced to surrender their passionately won gains and withdraw under cover of darkness.

THIEPVAL

32nd Division. Major-General WH Rycroft

36TH (ULSTER) DIVISION

SCHWABEN REDOUBT

THIEPVAL WOOD

32ND DIVISION

THIEPVAL

MOUQUET FARM

Leipzig Salient

Wonder Werk

Nab (Blighty) Valley

AUTHUILLE

Nordwerk

AUTHUILLE WOOD

The 32nd Division was for the most part New Army – enthusiastic Kitchener Volunteers from the autumn of 1914. The 'Big Push' here on the Somme was to be their first action. The Division comprised Pals Battalions from Salford and Manchester, Newcastle and Scotland. Their pioneers were the Newcastle Railway Pals. The divisional boundary with the 36th Ulsters was at the eastern corner of Thiepval Wood, and it was the 1st Salfords who occupied this far left flank of 32nd's front. Most of the them were second generation Irish Catholics, whose fathers had helped build the Manchester Ship Canal.

To the right of the Salford Pals were the Tyneside Commercials, composed mainly of the white-collar clerical classes of Newcastle. South of the Tyneside Commercials, opposite Leipzig Salient, was the Glasgow Boys' Brigade and the Glasgow Commercials. All these new boys were ranged against the experienced 99th Reserve Infantry

'I vividly remember Colonel Ritson standing in the British front line, tears streaming down his face, saying over and over,"My God! my boys, my boys!"'

Lance-Corporal S Henderson, Newcastle Commercials.

Troops advancing in a later attack on Thiepval.

Regiment, who had recently been 'stiffened' by the arrival of Major von Fabeck, a meticulous solder. Dugouts were made deeper and a complete extra system of defences added. Together with the imposing incline up to the German front line from Thiepval Wood, a strong position had become almost impregnable.

On 1 July, the Salford Pals and the Tyneside Commercials made a frontal assault against these monstrous defences. It was always going to be a hopeless, poignant failure. When the whistles sounded the Tommies climbed out of their trenches and began the steady walk up the hill, rifles at the port. Within minutes the bulk of their advance was halted in No Man's Land by a combination of enfilading machine-gun fire, rifle fire and artillery shells. In front of Thiepval hundreds of the men from Salford and Newcastle were killed. A mere handful of Salfords penetrated the German wire and made it into the Front

line trench, but nothing was heard of them again. The Tyneside Commercials were scythed down before even reaching the German Front line. The German defenders, having endured the indescribable agony of seven days of British artillery raining down shells upon them, were exaltant, standing on their trench parapets and waving the Geordies on so that they could pick them off with rifle fire. The attack at Thiepval was stopped as the disaster unfolded. The German artillery fired on No Man's Land throughout the day, and the wounded lay out there in the blistering midsummer heat.

When dusk fell, those that could crawled back to the British lines, whilst the agonies and wailing of those still alive but unable to move filled the air. 1 July would come to leave a deep scar on hundreds of close-knit communities back home, and for many years after the War's end, Salford remembered it simply as 'Thiepval Day'.

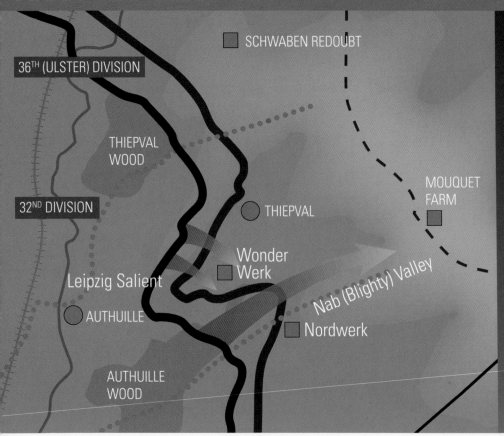

SCHWABEN REDOUBT

36TH (ULSTER) DIVISION

THIEPVAL
WOOD

MOUQUET
FARM

32ND DIVISION

THIEPVAL

Wonder
Werk

Leipzig Salient

Nab (Blighty) Valley

AUTHUILLE

Nordwerk

AUTHUILLE
WOOD

'As I approached the German trenches, I could see a wall of German soldiers standing shoulder-to-shoulder right along the parapet of their front-line trench, waving us to come on.'

Private L Ramage, Glasgow Boys' Brigade

To the south of Thiepval the Germans had obtained maximum tactical advantage from the long, sloping salient that extended out from Thiepval Ridge and the small valley that separated it from the Ovillers spur. Their front line followed the contours of the salient, then pulled back to the head of the valley. This was known to the British as The Nab, or Blighty Valley. The redoubt at the tip of the salient was the Granatloch, and set further back on the height of its slope was the Wonderwerk. On the hill to the south side of Blighty Valley was the Nordwerk, yet another machine-gun position which controlled any incursions up the valley. This hill was in the province of the British 8th Division's attack and was to be taken by their left flank.

The whole of the Leipzig Salient was to be knocked out from the west by the 16th and 17th Highland Light Infantry – the Glasgow Boys' Brigade and the Glasgow Commercials. Round the corner of the salient, men from the Cumbrian Lonsdale Battalion, together with the 1st Dorsets and 3rd Salford Pals were to come out of trenches in Authuille Wood and make their way up Blighty Valley, then on towards their objective of Mouquet Farm, up on Thiepval Ridge.

During the final moments of the hurricane bombardment, the Glasgow Commercials crept to within yards of the German line. When the barrage lifted, the Scots stormed into the Granatloch defences. To their left, the Glasgow Boys' Brigade did not fare so well. Their task was to overrun the Wonder Werk trenches, but they found the wire impenetrable and suffered heavy casualties from the machine-guns there. Again, as at Thiepval Fort, the German defenders stood on the parapet of their trench and mocked the attackers. At the Granatloch,

1. Present-day scene at the Granatloch position on Leipzig Salient.
2. View to the Nordwerk position, from the Lonsdales' trenches. The machine-guns were sited on the horizon in this picture.

 32nd Division. Major-General WH Rycroft

THE LEIPZIG SALIENT AND BLIGHTY VALLEY

companies of 2nd King's Own Yorkshire Light Infantry (KOYLI) joined with the Glasgow Commercials in consolidating this precious inroad. Later that morning, the Cumbrians launched their attack up Blighty Valley, in the expectation that the machine-gun emplacement at the Nordwerk had been taken. In a catastrophic error of command, they were allowed to continue their attack despite 32nd Division HQ being aware that 8th Division's attack south of them had failed. 'Before even reaching their jumping-off trenches, the Lonsdales had been destroyed by an enfilade machine-gun storm from the Nordwerk'

As if this communications error were not enough, it was fatally compounded by a further attack by the 1st Dorsets at exactly the same location, and with the same terrible consequences. In attempting to clamber over the bodies of the Lonsdales at the jumping off trenches,

the Dorsets were also decimated. Incredibly, yet a third attempt was made to attack up Blighty Valley, this time by the 3rd Salford Pals. Despite losing half their fighting strength in the attack, small parties of the Salfords were forced left and made it into the safety of the Granatloch that had been taken shortly after Zero Hour, and which was still being held by a dwindling force of Glasgow Commercials and 2nd KOYLI.

Sergeant Turnbull orchestrated the defence of this toehold in the German front line, although he did not make it to the end of the day. He was awarded a posthumous VC and is buried in the Lonsdale Cemetery close by the salient. Nevertheless, the Granatloch was held by the British from 1 July onwards.

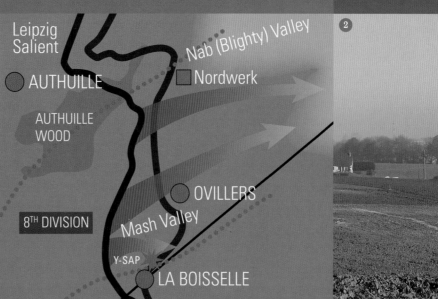

① Leipzig Salient

AUTHUILLE

AUTHUILLE WOOD

Nab (Blighty) Valley

Nordwerk ②

OVILLERS

8TH DIVISION

Mash Valley

Y-SAP

LA BOISSELLE

OVILLERS AND MASH VALLEY

■ 8th Division. Major General H Hudson

'Presently, the air cleared, and I could see what was happening. In the distance I saw the barrage, bounding on towards Pozières, the Third German Line, and in No Man's Land were heaps of dead, and Germans almost standing up in their trenches, well over the top, firing and sniping at those who had taken refuge in the shell holes...'

Captain Alan Hanbury-Sparrow, 8th Division.

1. Blighty Valley, looking towards the Nordwerk position, which destroyed the left flank of 8th Division's attack.

2. This panorama shows the extreme distance of No Man's Land near to La Boisselle; the photograph was taken from the British position, the German line occupying the lane which crosses the middle distance rising to the front of the village.

The 8th Division's attack front stretched south from Blighty valley down to the German-held village of Ovillers and into Mash Valley, where it met the divisional boundary of the 34th at La Boisselle. Their attack was characterized by the huge width of No Man's Land which some troops in the Division had to cross – over 750 yards in places.

When the Glasgow Commercials' of the 32nd Div took the Granatloch, over the hill on Leipzig Salient, German defenders were diverted and initially the left flank of 8th Division's attack proceeded successfully. New Army men of the 8th York & Lancs and the 8th KOYLI fought their way through three lines of German trenches just to the west of the Nordwerk. However, the following support troops of the 9th Yorks & Lancs then began to sustain heavy casualties from the worsening machine-gun fire from the Leipzig Salient. The forward troops in the German trenches were then surrounded by the defenders retaking their front line. These stranded men were unable to be reinforced by the 11th Sherwood Foresters, who suffered raking machine-gun fire in their attempts to get across No Man's Land. Further south, in the centre of 8th Division's

attack, three battalions of 23 Brigade attacking Ovillers were held up by withering machine-gun fire. Eventually, men of the 2nd Lincolns made the German front line, where they were marshalled by Lieutenant-Colonel Bastard into defending their gains. After holding on for an hour and a half, they were forced to retire back across No Man's Land, where they came across hundreds of dead and dying men.

On the right flank of 8th Division, 25 Brigade were faced with the greatest distance of No Man's Land across the whole of the British attack – the empty spaces of Mash Valley, north of La Boisselle. Their first task was to take the Albert-Bapaume Road, so that they could advance on Pozières, their final objective. In the event, Mash Valley immediately became a terrible killing field. The three attacking battalions made no inroads at all into the German Front line, except for a few men of 2nd Middlesex, who were quickly repelled. Casualties here in Mash Valley were dreadful. Accounts differ over the final total, but the 2nd Middlesex lost almost 600 men. 2nd Devons and 2nd West Yorks each lost over 400 men. The total casualties in 8th Division on 1 July were 5121. Nineteen hundred men were dead.

LA BOISSELLE

"I did see poor Aggy Fife [one of the Tyneside Scottish pipers]. He was riddled with bullets, writhing and screaming. Another lad was just kneeling, his head thrown right back. Bullets were just slapping into him, knocking great bloody chunks off his body."

Private J Elliot, Tyneside Scottish

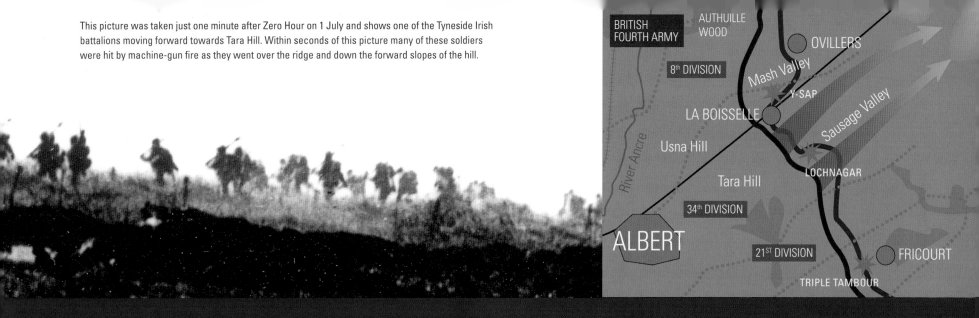

This picture was taken just one minute after Zero Hour on 1 July and shows one of the Tyneside Irish battalions moving forward towards Tara Hill. Within seconds of this picture many of these soldiers were hit by machine-gun fire as they went over the ridge and down the forward slopes of the hill.

BRITISH FOURTH ARMY
AUTHUILLE WOOD
OVILLERS
8th DIVISION
Mash Valley
Y-SAP
LA BOISSELLE
Sausage Valley
Usna Hill
River Ancre
LOCHNAGAR
Tara Hill
34th DIVISION
ALBERT
21ST DIVISION
FRICOURT
TRIPLE TAMBOUR

The 34th Division comprised two brigades of Northumberland Fusiliers – The Tyneside Scottish and the Tyneside Irish – and one brigade made up of the First and Second Edinburgh City battalions, the Cambridge Battalion, and the Grimsby Chums. All the Division's twelve battalions were deployed in the attack. They were to take the Front line village of La Boisselle, then strike further east into the German Second Position at Contalmaison. They were destined to be involved in 'some of the most cataclysmic, seminal moments' of British military history.

East out of the British-held town of Albert the land rises to a ridge, then falls away down the Tara-Usna hill into La Boisselle. On each side of the village were two shallow valleys, into which the main thrusts of the attack were to take place. Observation balloons were often flown in the southerly of the two, and thus to the Tommies this was "Sausage" Valley. Quite naturally, the corresponding valley to the north became "Mash" valley. Minutes before Zero Hour, two huge mines, one either side of La Boisselle, were to be detonated underneath the German front line. As well as destroying key gun emplacements, the mines would create huge 'lips' around the craters – excellent points from which to attack into the German line. To protect the troops from the effects of the massive explosions, they had been pulled back to their reserve trenches, but in places these were over 500 yards – more than half a kilometre – from the German front line.

At 7:28am the mines went up. First, one to the left of the village, Mash Valley – at Y Sap. Then an enormous one to the right, at Lochnagar: '...the detonation of the mines created both a spectacular outburst of flame and a gigantic plume of debris which gushed skywards in the most devastating and awesome cacophony of sound and shockwaves yet heard in warfare.' As the noise from a clutch of smaller explosions in the distance at Fricourt died away, a strange whining was heard – the Tyneside Scottish pipers were tuning up to play their soldiers into battle. At 7:30am the whistles went and 34th Division's assault on La Boisselle began. The troops poured out of their reserve trenches and began the long trek down the Tara-Usna slopes to the German front line. At first there was no response from the defenders, but they were merely allowing the advancing troops to reach a point of no return: 'You know Fritzie had let us come on just enough so that we were exposed coming down that slope. That way we would cop it if we came forward and cop it just as bad if we tried to go back. We were just scythed down. We found out later that they must have aimed at our thighs so that when we went down, we got hit again as we fell.'
Private J Elliot, Tyneside Scottish

►►

75

The Lochnagar Mine. Blown at 7:28 on the 1st of July, it made a huge crater which has been preserved today.

DEFENCE OF CRATERS.

16 m.   22 m.

TUNNEL   ← 60,000 lbs AMMORAL

LOCHNAGAR CRATER MEMORIAL

Detail of photograph taken in Le Tommy Bar, showing aerial view of the Lochnagar crater with added information.

"The whole earth heaved and flashed, and a tremendous and magnificent column rose up into the sky. There was an ear-splitting roar, drowning all the guns, flinging my aircraft sideways in the repercussing air. The earth column rose higher and higher to almost 4,000 feet. There it hung, or seemed to hang, for a moment in the air, like the silhouette of some great cypress tree, then fell away in a widening cone of dust and debris."

2nd Lieutenant CA Lewis, 3 Squadron RFC, from 'Sagittarius Rising'

The German machine-guns rattled relentlessly back and forth along the lines of steadily advancing men. The advancing lines were literally scythed as the machine-guns swept over them, the dead and wounded lying in orderly rows; any survivors from the first spray of bullets were dropped or finished off by successive sweeps.

The slopes of the Tara-Usna hills became covered with the dead and dying of the 34th. With the attack faltering badly, each following wave of men became held up by the one before, so that soldiers became bunched together, unsure of what to do or where to go to escape the onslaught. Extraordinarily, in Mash Valley, small parties of Tyneside Irish managed to evade the fire and enter the German front line trenches. In Sausage Valley, the Grimsby Chums had taken possession of the forward lip of the massive Lochnagar crater, still hot and stinking from the ammonial explosive used to blow it, and began to consolidate a crucial foothold in the German line. As the morning wore on, wounded and lost men made their way in. It soon became the main focus of fire for German defenders. 'I saw a man near me, shot through the head. He rolled over and over, right to the bottom of the crater.'
Corporal A Dickinson, Grimsby Chums.

Officer casualties at La Boisselle were also dreadful. In the 20th Battalion of the Tyneside Scottish, every Officer who had gone over was hit. Commanding Officer Lieutenant-Colonel C Sillery was killed. In the 23rd Battalion, Lieutenant-Colonel W Lyle was last seen alive with a walking stick in hand, amongst his men in No Man's Land. Most officers had been hit whilst leading their troops down the slopes, and before they had even reached the British forward trenches.

Within this monumental carnage two courageous feats should be noted: a small band of 2nd Edinburgh City men made it through the carnage to their final objective beyond La Boisselle, before being surrounded and most probably killed; and another separate party of Tyneside Irish, the remnants of the company who had got into the German front line, also fought their way through to Contalmaison before succumbing to the inevitable. Nevertheless, they had advanced the furthest of any unit on the battle front that day, covering almost two and a half miles, finally grinding to a mortal halt a mile inside the enemy lines.

77

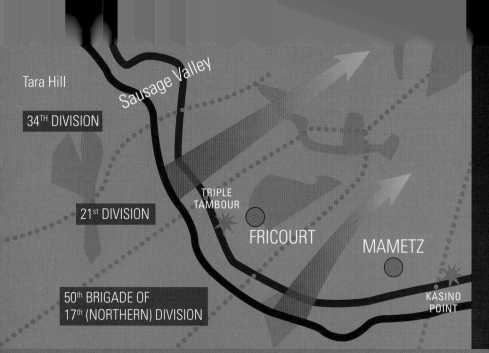

Tara Hill

34ᵀᴴ DIVISION

Sausage Valley

TRIPLE TAMBOUR

21ˢᵗ DIVISION

FRICOURT

MAMETZ

50ᵗʰ BRIGADE OF 17ᵗʰ (NORTHERN) DIVISION

KASINO POINT

 21st Division. Major-General DGM Campbell

 50th Brigade of 17th (Northern) Division. Major-General TD Pilcher

Barely discernible against the chalk spoil of the trenches, British troops go forward in the attack on Mametz on 1 July.

SUCCESS IN THE SOUTH

The terrain around Fricourt and Mametz made for particularly good defence, and the Germans had taken full advantage of it. Both villages had been fortified and were connected by a bewildering network of trenches. In places No Man's Land was less than a hundred yards wide. Fricourt was not to be attacked directly – the 21st Division would assault well to the left of the village, with the 7th Division attacking to the right of it. The garrison in Fricourt would then be isolated and could be attacked from both sides. A battalion of the 17th Division – the 10th West Yorks – was to participate in 21st Division's attack.

Around the area the defending German artillery had been well-targeted and to some extent silenced by British guns. At 7:28am three large mines were exploded underneath the German lines, destroying the German line opposite the British Tambour Salient on the left of Fricourt. They were blown to prevent machine-gun fire on the men of the 21st Division as they progressed to the left of Fricourt. However, the leading wave of 10th West Yorks were then shredded by machine guns from the Red Cottage area in the north of the village. They had the terrible distinction of sustaining the heaviest battalion losses across the whole of the British attack on 1 July – 688 men and 22 officers out of the 800 who attacked became casualties.

Despite this appalling slaughter, on their left, the 4th Middlesex and most of 64th Brigade progressed into the German lines north of the village. Major Loudoun-Shand of the 10th Green Howards won his VC here. They fought their way through to Crucifix Trench, where, despite German counter-attacks, they successfully held and consolidated their gains. ▶▶

79

7th Division. Major General HE Watts.

Six of the 7th Division battalions were New Army, with three Manchester Pals battalions, the Oldham Pals and the 2nd Gordon Highlanders. Other battalions included the 8th and 9th Devonshires and the 1st Royal Welch Fusiliers – the battalion of Second Lieutenant Siegfried Sassoon, the war poet and writer. The poet William Noel Hodgson was also in the 7th Division at Mametz. Best known for his poem 'Before Action', Hodgson was a company commander in the 9th Devonshires, in the leading wave at 7:30am.

7th Division was to attack the village of Mametz, and on its left flank the 9th Devons and 2nd Borders would attack out of their Mansel Copse positions over particularly difficult ground. Whilst on leave before the attack, another officer of the 9th Devons, Captain Duncan Martin, had amused himself by fashioning a plasticine model of the Devons' position and the No Man's Land they would have to cross. A German machine-gun position at The Shrine, south of the village, commanded full views of their route, and in the course of studying his model, Martin came to realise that he and his men would be cut down in their initial attack by this very position.

After the whistles went, the 22nd Manchesters (the 7th Pals) on the right of the attack progressed quickly despite machine-gun fire and inside thirty minutes had advanced to Bucket Trench, close to Danzig Alley. The 1st South Staffordshires meanwhile had reached the ruins of Mametz.

In the centre of the attack, the 2nd Gordons were initially held up by sustained fire from The Shrine, and on their left, the the 9th Devons suffered from this too – tragically, Captain Martin's deductions were well-founded, and at Mansel Copse the 9th Devons' attack was brought to a halt by it. Martin and Hodgson were both amongst the fatalities. By the afternoon, 7th Division had fought their way into the village and taken the trenches at Danzig Alley, and by the day's end Bunny Alley and Fritz Trench had been cleared of defenders and consolidated. The bodies of Martin and Hodgson were recovered from the battlefield and brought back to the trenches at Mansel Copse, where they were buried along with other fatalities from the 9th Devonshires.

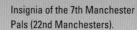

Insignia of the 7th Manchester Pals (22nd Manchesters).

'The Devonshires held this trench, the Devonshires hold it still'

Inscription by the entrance to the Devonshires' Cemetery in Mansel Copse

1. This panorama shows the landscape over which the left flank of the 7th Division attacked at Mametz. The extreme left of the picture shows Mansel Copse, from where the 9th Devons' attack came. The buildings are the eastern edge of Mametz village. The German front line begins below the buildings on the left and rises up and over the hill towards the middle of the picture. To the extreme right can be seen the Gordon Highlanders' cemetery, whose men attacked alongside the Devons.

2. Still from Geoffrey Malins' film of the battle, showing German prisoners being brought into Minden Post, Carnoy on 1 July.

81

SWEEPING THROUGH MONTAUBAN

18th (Eastern) Division. Major General FI Maxse

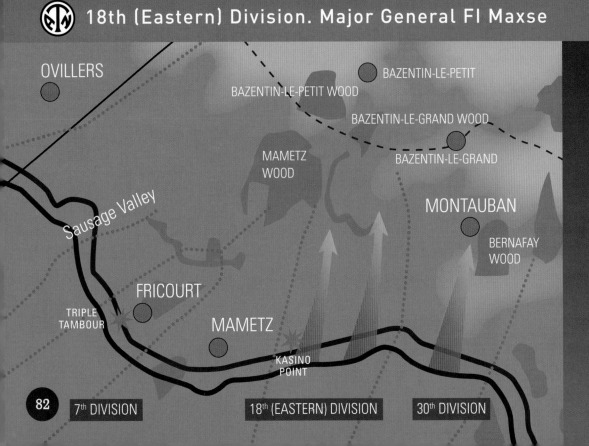

OVILLERS

BAZENTIN-LE-PETIT

BAZENTIN-LE-PETIT WOOD

BAZENTIN-LE-GRAND WOOD

BAZENTIN-LE-GRAND

MAMETZ WOOD

MONTAUBAN

Sausage Valley

BERNAFAY WOOD

FRICOURT

TRIPLE TAMBOUR

MAMETZ

KASINO POINT

7th DIVISION

18th (EASTERN) DIVISION

30th DIVISION

'As the gunfire died away I saw an infantryman climb onto the parapet into No Man's Land, beckoning others to follow. As he did so he kicked off a football; a good kick, the ball rose and travelled well towards the German line. That seemed to be the signal to advance.'

Private LS Price, 8th Royal Sussex

'War such as this, on such a beautiful day, seems to me to be quite correct and proper.'

Private R Cude, 7th East Kents

German prisoners being marched back to the British lines.

The successful attacks in the south vividly demonstrated several aspects of the British strategy. They showed in the first instance that a properly conducted bombardment, with the deadly accurate heavy French guns lending their weight, was unanswerable. They also showed that divisional-level initiatives which departed from "the dead hand of Fourth Army centralisation" could make a difference between achievement and bloody failure.

18th Division's Commander was Major General Ivor Maxse, an inspiring leader. His philosophy was to ensure that nothing would be left to chance. The 18th Division was to attack to the left of Montauban, and they dug a series of 'Russian Saps' out to within twenty yards of the German front line. (A 'Russian Sap' was a trench-like tunnel dug below ground level which could quickly be opened at the surface at any required time.) On the nights leading up to the attack, Maxse's troops launched trench raids to ascertain the bombardment's effectiveness, taking prisoners and "procuring" information.

At Zero, two large mines were exploded – one under Kasino Point – destroying key machine-gun positions. The 18th Division went over, and by 10:15 that morning the entire width of the assault had reached the third trenches in the front line.

The advance of the 8th East Surreys into No Man's Land had featured one of the Somme's most famous exploits. Whilst on leave, Captain WP 'Billy' Nevill had bought four footballs, and offered a prize to the first man in the battalion to kick one into the German front line. Whatever his motives, the ex-public schoolboy's actions had the desired effect, and the East Surreys and 7th Queen's went over singing and shouting, kicking the balls onwards towards the Germans. Nevill himself affected a nonchalent air, smoking a cigarette as he made his way across No Man's Land. Cruelly, he was fatally hit when almost upon the German wire. Montauban Alley, the extensive trench system behind the village and 18th Division's second objective, was taken and secured by the end of the day. ▶▶

British gunners loading an 18-pounder field gun in the Carnoy Valley at Montauban.

'The only feeling I had was to get to the objective and stay there and the thought that was uppermost in my mind was the phrase "for England", which I seemed to be repeating continually. This is the truth and not put in for heroics. To be perfectly truthful, I was scared stiff.'

Private WLP Dunn, 1st Liverpool Pals

 ## 30th Division. Major-General JSM Shea

The 30th Division were on the privileged right flank of the British attack, next to the experienced French Sixth Army. Their target was the fortified village of Montauban, some way beyond the Front line. This was a New Army division containing Pals Battalions from Liverpool and Manchester. The 1st Liverpool Pals were, in fact, the first of all the Pals Battalions, raised by Lord Derby, the prominent MP of the time. The formation of the Liverpool Pals was closely followed by the raising of the Manchester Pals – the rivalry between them was keen even in 1914. The 30th Division contained four battalions of Pals from each of these two great cities of the north west. The other battalions in the 30th were the 2nd Royal Scots Fusiliers, the 2nd Wiltshires, the 2nd Green Howards and the 2nd Bedfords.

The German wire in front of 30th Division had been destroyed in the barrage and none of the leading wave encountered difficulties – most of the defenders were caught in their dugouts, and little resistance was offered. By 8:30am two battalions of the Liverpool Pals had attacked and taken Dublin Trench and had joined up with the French on their right, who were also making quick progress. The Liverpool Pals were supported by the 2nd Bedfords, mopping up behind them. By 10am, progressing under cover of smoke, the Manchesters and Royal Scots Fusiliers had entered Montauban village, only to find it deserted – the defenders were retreating in large numbers. The 1st Manchester Pals then successfully rushed the artillery battery beyond the village in Caterpillar Valley to capture the first field guns of the day – and Montauban had been consolidated.

Just after midday the 4th Liverpool Pals captured the Division's final objective – La Briquetèrie, south of Bernafay Wood. The attack had been an unqualified success, but yet, even in this cleanest of victories, casualties totalled more than 3000.

THE FRENCH ATTACK

A heavy French rail gun.

As the barrage died, and through an early morning mist, the French forces advanced alongside the British 30th Division, carrying all before them.

The French sector of the Somme, now much truncated because of their parlous situation at Verdun, stretched from the 30th Division's boundary south-east of Montauban, southwards astride the Somme. Their overall objectives were to take the German Second Position at Maurepas, down to Flaucourt, opposite Peronne. On 1 July the French chose to limit their objectives to the German front line, and the German defences south of the River Somme were not as imposing, as at Thiepval and the Schwaben Redoubt. They also had the benefit of battle-hardened troops and an extremely powerful and accurate artillery, and with more than enough guns to achieve their objectives.

The French attack was carried out by the Sixth Army, under General Fayolle. The XX Corps, next to the British 30th Division at Montauban, attacked at 07:30, and powered forward alongside their British Allies. They completely overran the entire German front line north of the River Somme, and probably, with their troops' experience, helped to pull the British 30th Division along with them.

South of the river the attack was delayed for two hours, a necessary turn of events, but one which seems genuinely to have surprised the German defenders. In this sector, the French I Colonial Corps and the XXXV Corps held utter dominance with their artillery. The German batteries were almost completely destroyed. When their attack did get under way, they carried all before them, sweeping imperiously through the Front line and consolidating their positions close to the German Second Position.

British dead on the battlefield.

AFTER THE TRAUMA

'This trench was full of dead Germans and they'd been there for some time…They were all different colours, from pallid grey to green and black. And they were bloated - that's how a corpse goes in time, they get blown up with gases.'

Corporal Clifford Lane, 1st Battalion, Hertfordshire Regiment

 17th Division.   **9th Division.**   **19th Division.**

In the fog of war, and with the inevitable rupture of communications, it didn't become immediately obvious to the High Command of the magnitude of the disaster that had befallen them, but to the troops at the sharp end, the carnage was everywhere. Numbers at roll-calls all along the front soon told the British High Command that their huge attack – the greatest offensive the British Army had ever planned and carried out – so carefully crafted, so meticulously planned, had failed, and had failed catastrophically. At Gommecourt, at Serre, along the Redan Ridge down to Beaumont Hamel, on the Schwaben Redoubt, at Thiepval, Blighty Valley, Ovillers, La Boisselle, and at Fricourt. All along the line No Man's Land was strewn with the dead of a Citizen Army which had been mutilated and broken on the back of a more powerful and vastly more experienced opponent. 19,240 men were dead. 35,493 had been wounded. 2152 were missing. 585 had been taken prisoner. And for hundreds of towns and villages back home, 1 July 1916 would never be forgotten.

What could Haig possibly do? There was no political way of cancelling the offensive – the French would never allow that. They needed the British to be fighting Germany on similar terms, and the battle had now been well and truly joined. The British had begun to pay the 'butcher's bill'. And, after all, there had been some success. The only possible thing that Haig and the British Army could do was to build on the day's gains, and carry on...

Very early on 2 July, as thousands of wounded Tommies were still attempting to crawl back to their own lines under cover of darkness, two separate British patrols entered Fricourt and took more than 100 prisoners. By noon the village was secured and by midnight the line had been pushed up to beyond Fricourt Wood. The eastern end of Montauban Alley was also secured. On 3 July, 9th Division took Bernafay Wood, to the right of Montauban, almost unopposed. At La Boisselle, the line had held beyond Lochnagar Crater since 1 July, and inroads were made into trenches on the edge of the village. The 13th Battalion of The Rifle Brigade were able to carry out battlefield clearance at La Boisselle and threw over 1000 of the 1 July dead into the Lochnagar Crater.

Fresh attacks were made on Ovillers and Thiepval, by the 12th and 32nd Divisions. Both of these divisions were now under the command of General Gough and the Reserve Army. At Ovillers, the men of 12th Division had relieved the shattered 8th, though they were under no illusion now as to the nature of what awaited them. And at Thiepval, instead of the large attack of three divisions initially envisaged, just two brigades attempted to storm the citadel. These attacks were disastrous, and from both operations few men returned unscathed, though on the afternoon of 4 July 19th Division succeeded in a three day operation to clear La Boisselle and some of the trenches running north towards Ovillers.

'The trenches became knee-deep, in some places waist-deep, in clinging slime, and, under shellfire, collapsed beyond recognition. Movement was almost an agony: men fainted from sheer exhaustion whilst struggling through deep mud...'

British Official History

CONTALMAISON

 19th Division   23rd Division   17th (Northern) Division

With the 1 July capture of the German front line at Mametz and Montauban, Rawlinson had begun to devise a wide attack north from here into the German Second Position up on Bazentin Ridge. As a prelude to this ambitious plan, several obstacles were to be taken first, clearing the way. They were: Contalmaison, beyond La Boisselle; positions in Mametz Wood, below Bazentin-le-Petit Wood; and Trones Wood and Hardecourt, in the south-east of the British sector. Ovillers, immediately to the north of La Boisselle was also included in these preliminary operations. All the attacks on 7 July were divisionally-controlled, which meant they each had their own jumping-off schedules.

Three separate divisions attacked in the direction of Contalmaison on 7th July. 19th Division on the left flank at 8:15am; 23rd Division at 10am; and 17th (Northern) Division, attacking from the direction of Fricourt. Their attack was timed to start in total darkness at 2am that morning.

The weather on 7 July was dreadful, with prolonged heavy rain. Despite this, the attack went ahead. In the torrential showers, parties

of Lancashire Fusiliers got as far as the outlying ruins of Contalmaison, but were repelled by strong German counter-attacks. 19th Division's attack had been successful. Starting at 8:15, by 10am that morning they had achieved their objective, taking over 400 prisoners in the process. The 1st Worcesters of 23rd Division, following through their leading waves at 10am, fought their way into Contalmaison but, disastrously, the weather brought their advance to a standstill, and German artillery gradually forced their withdrawal.

In the 17th Division's sector, 12th Manchesters and 9th Duke of Wellington's had attacked again at 8am, but were caught out in the open by heavy machine-gun fire from Mametz Wood. The 12th Manchesters sustained horrific casualties – a total of 555 officers and men. By 8pm that day, the appalling weather conditions and incessant German artillery fire caused all attacks to be cancelled.

By the next morning, 8 July, the mud was so deep the men could hardly move. The 1st Worcesters tried again to take the village, but were

Sappers clearing rubble in Contalmaison in order to build a road, shortly after the battle.

forced to withdraw by heavy shell-fire. The morning after, 9 July, a machine-gun post was established south of Contalmaison, which gave effective control over the area, and by evening Bailiff Wood, to the west of Contalmaison, had been taken by the 12th Durham Light Infantry. All was now set for the capture of the village, which was ordered for the next day. The attack was made by the 8th and 9th Battalions of the Yorkshire Regiment (the Green Howards), together with two companies of the 11th West Yorks attacking from Bailiff Wood. Despite incurring shrapnel and machine-gun fire whilst crossing a long stretch of open ground, the 8th and 9th Yorkshires took the first trench on the west of the village in a bayonet charge, causing the surviving Germans to retreat into the ruined village. Captured machine-guns were turned on the fleeing Germans. After a series of short skirmishes the Yorkshiremen took a total of 268 prisoners. The attack from Bailiff Wood was also successful, with the 11th West Yorks meeting up with the Green Howards to complete the capture. It had come though, with another grim cost in men – total casualties of 23rd Division over the four days were 3845 officers and men.

'Everybody for themselves. The brambles; trees falling...our main concern was keeping alive. They wouldn't come too close to me with the Lewis gun. I was going along firing from the hip. We managed to drive them out...'

Private George Richards, 13th Battalion, Welch Regiment, 38th Division

THE WELSH TAKE MAMETZ WOOD

 38th (Welsh) Division

The 38th (Welsh) Division attacked from Happy Valley into the southern edge of Mametz Wood at 8:30am on Friday, 7 July. The 16th Welch and 11th South Wales Borderers were the first two battalions to go over. They had to cross a considerable distance of No Man's Land, and at first it seemed as though the bombardment had done its job. There was no enemy fire. However, 50 yards from the wood, the Germans launched a hail of machine-gun fire on both battalions from carefully hidden positions. The 16th Welch Regiment was cut to ribbons, and the South Wales Borderers hardly fared any better.

After being reinforced by the 10th South Wales Borderers, another attempt was made to enter the wood, but the merciless machine-gun fire completely stopped them in their tracks. The brigade was withdrawn and an attempt was made early the next morning, 8 July, under cover of darkness, to enter the southern salient, although this

too broke down because of thick German wire and the boggy ground conditions. It was impossible to make any progress.

Two days later, on 10 July at 4:15am, an attack was launched from White Trench. Under cover of the bombardment and smoke, 14 Brigade led the attack and the wood was reached. After digging in, the supporting troops of 113 Brigade joined them, and they rallied to their first objective. By 6am they had progressed well into the wood. From there, indecisive fighting took place until the early afternoon, when three companies of 17th Welsh Fusiliers arrived in support. The 38th's attack slowly and eventually pushed the Germans back to the northern edge of the wood, but the vicious fighting continued until 12 July, when the wood was finally cleared and consolidated. Over the course of five days, the 38th Division suffered casualties amounting to 3993 men, but the first wood in 'the Horseshoe' had been taken.

The resplendent memorial to the 38th Welsh Division at Mametz wood

MAMETZ
WOOD
1916

The Great Horseshoe of Woods is a convenient shorthand term usually ascribed to Martin Middlebrook and used to describe the principle areas of the fighting on the Somme following 1 July. It usually includes, from bottom left working clockwise: Mametz Wood; Bazentin-le-Petit Wood; Bazentin-le-Grand Wood; High Wood; Delville Wood; Trones Wood, and Bernafay Wood.

AUTHUILLE

AUTHUILLE WOOD

POZIERES

OVILLERS

CONTALMAISON

LA BOISSELLE

FRICOURT

River Ancre

ALBERT

KEY

▬▬▬▬	ALLIED FRONT LINE 1 JULY
▪▪▪▪▪	ALLIED FRONT LINE DAWN 14 JULY
··········	ALLIED POSITIONS EVENING 14 JULY
▬▬▬▬	GERMAN FRONT LINE 1 JULY
▪▪▪▪	GERMAN SECOND POSITION
▪▪▪▪▪▪	GERMAN THIRD POSITION
◢	THE GREAT HORSESHOE OF WOODS
◣	OTHER WOODS
⬤	TOWN / VILLAGE
▬▬▬	ROAD
┼┼┼┼	RAILWAY

0   0.5   1

1 Mile

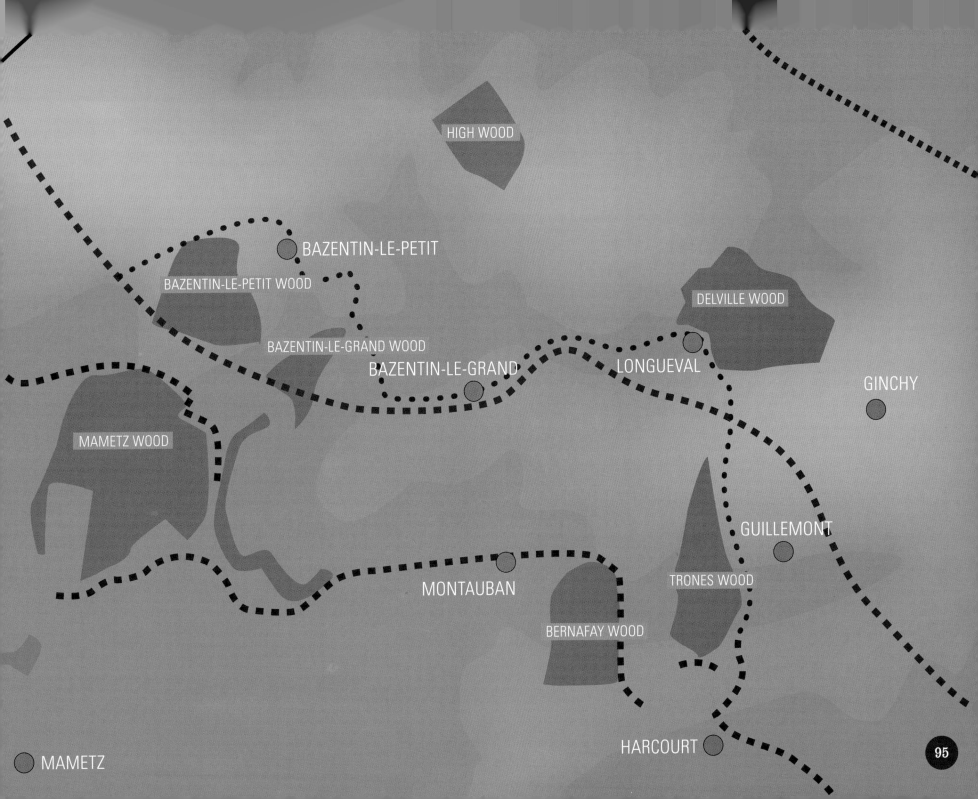

HIGH WOOD

BAZENTIN-LE-PETIT

BAZENTIN-LE-PETIT WOOD

DELVILLE WOOD

BAZENTIN-LE-GRAND WOOD

BAZENTIN-LE-GRAND

LONGUEVAL

GINCHY

MAMETZ WOOD

GUILLEMONT

MONTAUBAN

TRONES WOOD

BERNAFAY WOOD

HARCOURT

MAMETZ

A panorama of 'The Great Horseshoe of Woods' taken from the British position north of Montauban.

THE DAWN ATTACK

The Dawn Attack inaugurated a series of coordinated assaults against a cluster of woods which straddled the German Second Line at the southern end of the British sector of the Somme front.

 18th (Eastern) Division

 9th (Scottish) Division

 21st Division

 7th Division

 3rd Division

After the horror of 1 July, Rawlinson and Lt.-Gen. Sir Walter Congreve devised a boldly different attack. Its objective would be a large length of the German Second Position along the Bazentin Ridge, from Bazentin Le Petit and its wood on the left, down to Longueval, by Delville Wood, on the right. A simultaneous assault by XV Corps on the left, under Lt.-Gen. Horne, comprising 7th and 21st Divisions, and XIII Corps, under Congreve, comprising 9th and 3rd Divisions, was planned. They would assemble silently under the cover of darkness close to the German defences. An intense bombardment of only five minutes' duration would then herald the rush on the trenches.

Haig, still of the opinion that the men were too inexperienced to attempt such a sophisticated operation, argued against it. Rawlinson, however, with the support of the corps commanders, stuck out for it, and Haig gave way, with the proviso that Trones Wood, to the right of the proposed attack, was finally taken prior to the main attack. 30th Division had attacked into the wood three days before, but the Germans were putting up stiff resistance. Maxse's 18th (Eastern) Division were detailed to relieve the 30th Division and finally clear Trones Wood.

At 3:25am the barrage stopped and the infantry attacked. The bombardment had been extremely effective: most of the German wire was destroyed, and so were the German trenches. Many of the defenders had been killed, and those that were left were completely caught out by the sudden massed infantry attack. This time there were no long lines of soldiers slowly advancing in broad daylight. Instead, thousands of troops managed to assemble close to the German lines without alerting any of the defenders.

On the left of the attack, the 6th, 7th and 8th Leicesters of 21st Division took Bazentin-le-Petit Wood in the first thirty-five minutes of the attack starting; The 2nd Borders and 9th Devons of 7th Division, who had sustained tragic casualties early on 1 July, took Bazentin-le-Grand Wood; to their right, after initially being held up at the wire, 3rd Division took the village of Bazentin-le-Grand, and on the far right of the main attack, the Scots of 9th Division were into the southern fringe of Delville Wood without a shot being fired. By 10am they had taken the village of Longueval. Next to them, the 18th Division had by this time also cleared Trones Wood.

Amidst the general jubilation at Fourth Army Headquarters came even more stirring news: Patrols sent over the ridge into the shallow valley that led to High Wood could not find a German in sight. They had evacuated High Wood. The Commanders of 3rd and 7th Divisions even went to see for themselves, and came excitedly hurrying back to contact Fourth Army HQ. ▶▶

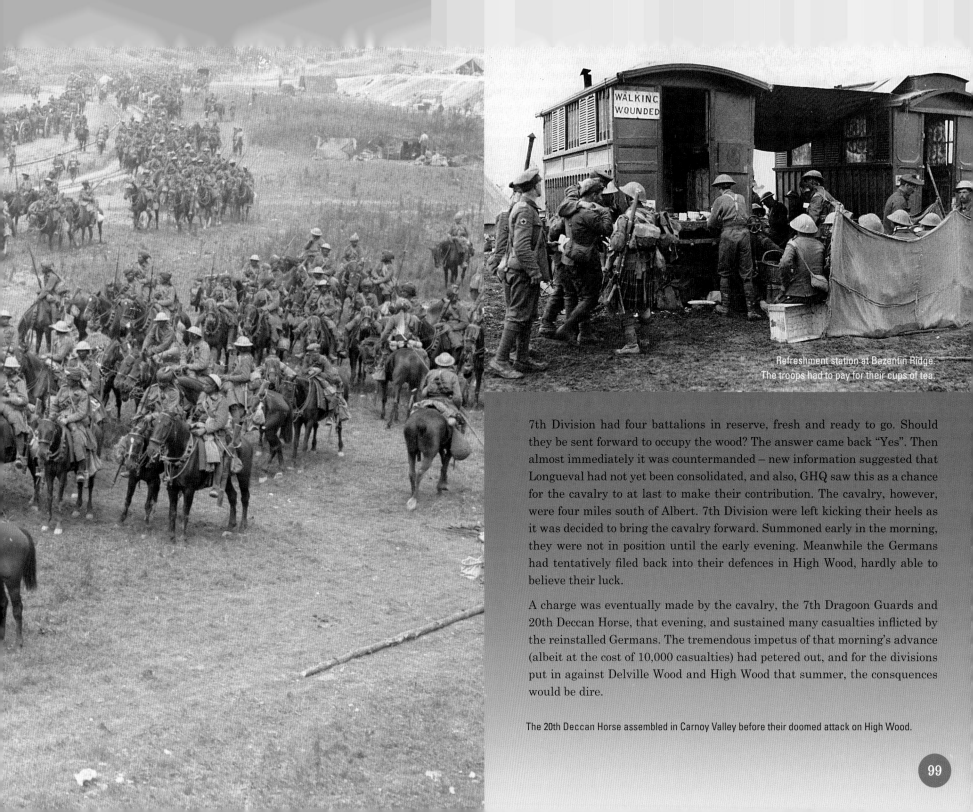

Refreshment station at Bazentin Ridge.
The troops had to pay for their cups of tea.

7th Division had four battalions in reserve, fresh and ready to go. Should they be sent forward to occupy the wood? The answer came back "Yes". Then almost immediately it was countermanded – new information suggested that Longueval had not yet been consolidated, and also, GHQ saw this as a chance for the cavalry to at last to make their contribution. The cavalry, however, were four miles south of Albert. 7th Division were left kicking their heels as it was decided to bring the cavalry forward. Summoned early in the morning, they were not in position until the early evening. Meanwhile the Germans had tentatively filed back into their defences in High Wood, hardly able to believe their luck.

A charge was eventually made by the cavalry, the 7th Dragoon Guards and 20th Deccan Horse, that evening, and sustained many casualties inflicted by the reinstalled Germans. The tremendous impetus of that morning's advance (albeit at the cost of 10,000 casualties) had petered out, and for the divisions put in against Delville Wood and High Wood that summer, the consquences would be dire.

The 20th Deccan Horse assembled in Carnoy Valley before their doomed attack on High Wood.

'I was sent back with five or six men to collect the pay books of our dead from 1 July. We had to turn them over to get to their breast pockets where they always kept their pay book, collected them in sandbags. We were face to face with the absolute horror of war – men decapitated, empty brain cavities, entrails where they'd been disembowelled. There was a corpse every odd yard, halfway up the seven hundred yards – very few of them got past that because they were being mowed down by machine-gun fire. In fact that day at Ovillers is absolutely engraved on my brain. I've thought about it all my life.'

Corporal Arthur Razzell, 8th Battalion, Royal Fusiliers, 12th Division

OVILLERS FINALLY FALLS

♠ **12th Division**

♣ **32nd Division**

♦ **48th Division**

The 13th Royal Fusilliers relaxing after their capture of a German trench on 8 July

O n 3 July, 12th Division had suffered a disastrous attack on Ovillers. They had lost 2400 officers and men. A further attack on 7 July was more successful, this time taking and holding German trenches on the western edge, and capturing a great number of prisoners, but again 12th Division sustained heavy casualties – over 1400 killed or wounded. At Haig's insistence another attack to capture the village was put in hand for the next day, 8 July. As at Contalmaison, the weather was awful, and 12th Division's attack was mired in deep mud – although progress was made into the village. In the evening, 74th Brigade renewed its attack on the southern edge of the village and made considerable progress. However, 12th Division was exhausted – they had been at Ovillers since the early morning of 2 July – and were in the process of being relieved by 14 Brigade of 32nd Division.

Since then, little progress had been made, despite many attempts, to finally capture the village. Hundreds of men had been expended in small,

'piecemeal' attacks between 9–14 July, and concern was expressed at High Command over their uncoordinated nature. On the night of 13 July various battalions were put in from practically every side to put an end to it. The village was almost surrounded, but owing to the churned terrain had become nearly unassailable. Its final defence by the German 2nd/15th Reserve Regiment was, however, a brave feat of endurance.

By 15 July Ovillers was still holding out – from the 32nd Division in the south-west, and 25th Division from the north-east, east and south. 32nd Division was relieved at nightfall by 144 Brigade of the 48th Division. From 1am on 16 July fighting began again and continued throughout the rest of the day, before, finally, two German officers and 126 soldiers surrendered. Next morning, 17 July, 300 yards of the original German front line north of Ovillers were also taken by 48th Division, after the Germans, who were in danger of being completely cut off, had retreated, leaving behind 80 of their wounded.

101

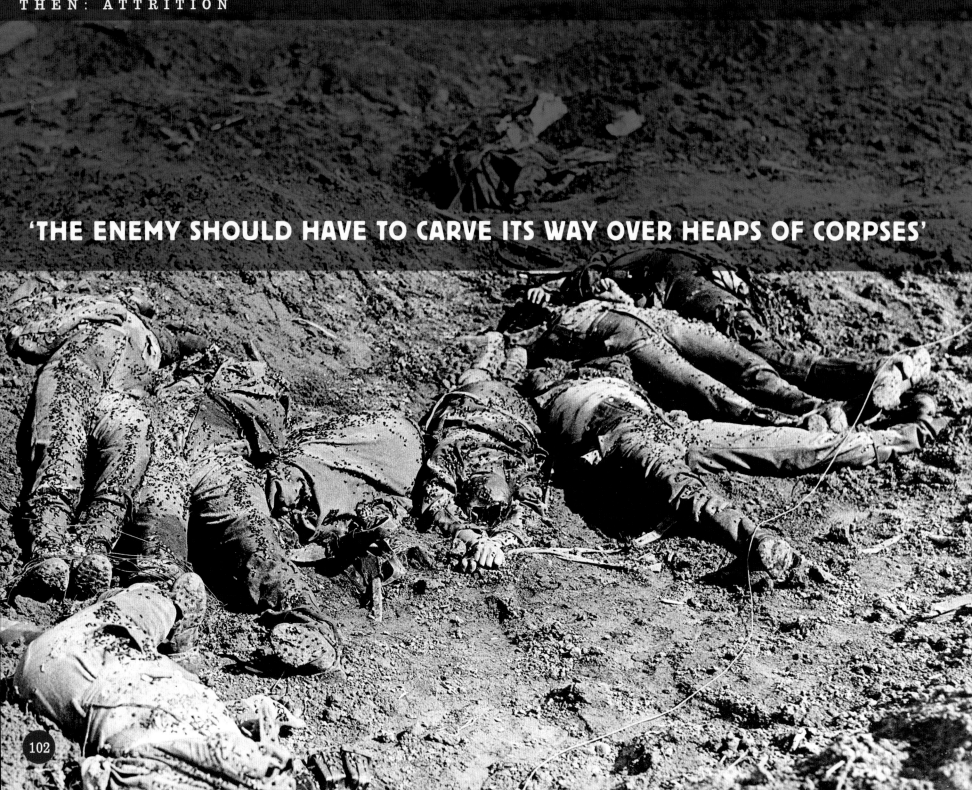

'THE ENEMY SHOULD HAVE TO CARVE ITS WAY OVER HEAPS OF CORPSES'

With pressure mounting on the Somme, by mid-July Falkenhayn had halted major operations against Verdun, one of the central objectives of the Allied campaign.

"HALTEN, WAS ZU HALTEN IST!"

HOLD ON TO WHATEVER CAN BE HELD

German rallying call

Despite the general British failure to achieve their planned objectives on the first day on the Somme, they had broken the German First Position in a number of places, and since then significant advances had been made. The success of the Dawn Attack had shaken the Germans, and they reorganized the structure of their armies across the entire Somme front. Reinforcements hardened the defences opposite the Bazentin Ridge, and the effect of this was soon to be felt by the British troops attacking into Delville Wood.

Falkenhayn, the German Commander-in-Chief, had laid down his philosophy to his army – 'it is a principle in trench warfare not to abandon a foot of ground and, if a foot is lost, to put in the last man to recover it by an immediate counter-attack', a

sentiment echoed by General F von Below: 'The enemy should have to carve its way over heaps of corpses.' This principle was largely responsible for the ferocious and attritional nature of the Somme. For each new advance made by the Allies, the Germans determined to take it back.

After 1 July, seven new German divisions were sent to the Somme, and two weeks into the campaign the German High Command suspended any further significant offensive operations at Verdun, although fighting continued until December, generally in France's favour. By the end of August, a further 40 German divisions had arrived on the Somme. As Joffre might have observed, it appeared that the British were now pulling their weight in the coalition.

FIGHTING FOR DEVIL'S WOOD

In this dreadful period of attrition, less ground was captured and Fourth
Army's casualties were 40 per cent greater than on the disaster of 1 July.

The 'Springboks' Brigade sustained 2300 dead in the bitter tug-of-war to control the Devil's Wood. They had paid the Devil's price.

On 14 July, the Scots of 9th Division had fought their way into the southern edge of Delville Wood. It seemed then that a significant advance beyond the Bazentin Ridge was there for the taking, but in the event, Delville Wood, the ruined village of Longueval, and High Wood became scenes of utter hell for two long months. The period between 14 July and 15 September was characterised by small-scale, piecemeal attacks, which resulted in a staggering number of casualties – around 82,000 – for very little ground gained.

By 17 July, 9th (Scottish) Division had consolidated Waterlot Farm, south of Delville Wood, and the South African Brigade were brought into the line to take the wood. Together, the 'Jocks' and the 'Springboks' hammered away at the Delville Wood and Longueval defences for three days. The South Africans took much of the wood in the first two hours, but continual German counter-attacks to retake the positions led to ferocious fighting which dragged on and on. 3rd Division attacked Longueval from the west and were able to make contact with the South Africans, who were then at the northern edge of Delville Wood. On 19 July 53 Brigade of the 18th Division claimed again the southern part of the wood. On 20 July, 3rd Division again attacked Delville Wood, but the 2nd Suffolks were almost entirely wiped out.

This deadly pattern, of taking and re-taking of the same ground, continued, with the 5th and 17th Divisions taking their turn in the line, until 27 August, when 'The Devil's Wood' was finally cleared and held. Less than a mile away, however, in this cauldron of woods, a similar tumultuous struggle had also been taking place, and it would cost a further two weeks of slaughter on both sides before the British were finally able to drive the German defenders from it.

THE BATTLE FOR
HIGH WOOD

'I saw men in their madness bayonet each other without mercy, without thought...I saw men torn to fragments by the near explosions of bombs, and – worse than any sight – I heard the agonised cries and shrieks of men in mortal pain who were giving up their souls to their Maker...the cries of those poor, tortured and torn men I can never forget. They are with me always.'

Corporal MJ Guiton, Civil Service Rifles, London Regiment, 47th Division

High Wood became a scene of unspeakable carnage. Like Delville Wood, the land resembled an almost prehistoric Hell. trees were devastated, ripped to bare trunks. The ground was poisoned, blasted, churned over and over as it was pounded time and again by shellfire, the battlefield dead blown to pieces and scattered across the cratered landscape. In the high summer of the Somme, flies bred horribly, so that they hung in huge menacing clouds over the battlefield. Rats were everywhere, bloated by feeding on the rotting parts of corpses. It shocked even the most battle-hardened of men.

The enormity of the horror to which thousands of men were subjected is grotesquely illuminated by the fact that on 14 July, after the success of the Dawn Attack, High Wood was empty and there for the taking. As we have seen, this opportunity was declined. Consequently, over an utterly desolate, forlorn and futile seven-week period, a total of ten divisions were rotated in and out of the line there. Haig's dictum to each was, of course, to 'take High Wood', although Fourth Army was still employing its bad old habits of piecemeal attacks. Pieces of trench were gradually nibbled away here and there, but the cost in men and morale was exhorbitant. Any advances were usually quickly reversed by strong German counter-attacks that swept the British back to their starting points. Summer dissolved into autumn, and by the time the next major attack was gearing up, High Wood was still there, its defenders grimly hanging on. On 15 September, as part of the general attack on Flers and Courcelette, 47th London Division finally took the prize. In III Corps area, High Wood was the key, for German machine-gun positions in the wood would severely hinder the progress of troops passing either side of it. With the Londoners dug in and engaged chaotically in many areas of the wood, the introduction of a relatively new type of weapon may have swung the fight in their favour. German machine-gun positions were hit with Stokes Trench Mortars. German survivors of these shattering detonations began to surrender rapidly. By the end of the day, the battered 47th London Division had made it through the wood north to Starfish Trench.

'ADVANCE AUSTRALIA – IF YOU CAN!'

Sign hung outside German trenches, greeting the Australian 5th Division at Fromelles, 19 July 1916

THE AUSTRALIANS AT

POZIERES

The Australians had arrived in France in March, 1916. Together with the New Zealanders, they had already earned a formidable reputation at Gallipoli. The Australian 5th Division was the first of the ANZACs to see action on the Western Front, at Fromelles, north of the Somme, on 19 July. On their arrival there, they were confronted with a sign hung outside the Germans' trenches: "Advance Australia – if you can!", which of course was promptly shot to bits.

Fromelles had been a disaster, and after Gallipoli, the Australians' opinion of the British Command went even further downhill. Their bitter experience at Pozières was not to change their minds. The Australian 1st Division was assigned to take the German Second Position at Pozières, as part of a multi-divisional night attack. Taking the village and the ridge upon which it stood – the highest point on the Somme – would open up the German position and give the Allies a 'back-door' route north to Thiepval. They would attack the village from the direction of Contalmaison in the south.

For this, their first assault, Divisional Command had consulted extensively with their British counterparts and attempted to learn from their recent fighting experience. Thus a combined operation was developed: on the Australians' left, north of the Albert-Bapaume Road, the 48th (South Midland) Division was to attack from the west and meet up with the Australians in the captured village.　▶▶

Australian troups manning a 'Flying Pig'
a 9.45-inch trench mortar, south of Pozières.

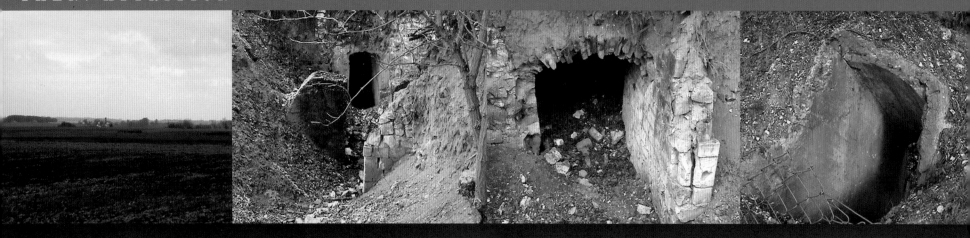

'Without doubt Pozières was the heaviest, bloodiest, rottenest stunt that ever the Australians were caught up in. The carnage was just indescribeable. As we were making our attack after the 3rd Brigade had gone through we were literally walking over the dead bodies of our cobbers that had been slain by this barrage.'

Private Frank Brent, 2nd Australian (New South Wales) Battalion, 1st Australian Division

Pozières was bombarded heavily for four days prior to the attack, and the Australians went in at half past midnight on 23 July. Creeping up into No Man's Land, 1 NSW Brigade and 3 Brigade stormed through Pozières Trench and by 1am were fighting to take the Albert-Bapaume road through the village. On their right flank, 9th (Queensland) Battalion were held up by the German OG1 and OG2 lines.

The Australians' reputation for tenacity and courage was cemented at Pozières, for the fighting was of a particularly bitter intensity. It was here that Private John Leak rushed a machine-gun position and killed the entire crew, for which he won his VC. By 3am four battalions were on the road and dug-in. After consolidating, the Aussies then attacked and took 'Gibraltar', the main German defensive position in the village. Their strong progress into the village, however, was not mirrored by 48th Division, whose attack had not gone well. Battalions of the Gloucesters from both 144 and 145 Brigades were mown down by fierce fire on their initial crossing of No Man's Land. On the right of 48th

Division's attack though, the 1/4th Oxfordshire and Buckinghamshire Light Infantry and 1/4th Royal Berkshires succeeded in capturing trenches close to the village.

All this time, the Aussies were being shelled constantly, and on their right flank the Germans launched the first of many counter-attacks from the OG trenches. This was beaten off, but the German artillery was beginning register with deadly accuracy: 'As fast as one portion of trench was cleared another was blown in. There were no dugouts in which we could take shelter – the only thing to do was grin and bear it. The shells, which were falling almost perpendicularly, could be clearly seen in the last forty feet of their descent, and the whole trench was methodically dealt with.' **Capt. JRO Harris, 3rd Australian (NSW) Bn, 1st Australian Division.** For the rest of that day, the Germans fired shell upon shell onto the village. It was a ruined wasteland. The Gibraltar position was the only building left standing. ▶▶

Above: The remains of the heavily-fortified German positio at 'Gibraltar', Pozières.

Members of the Royal Army Medical Corps
dressing a German prisoner's wounds

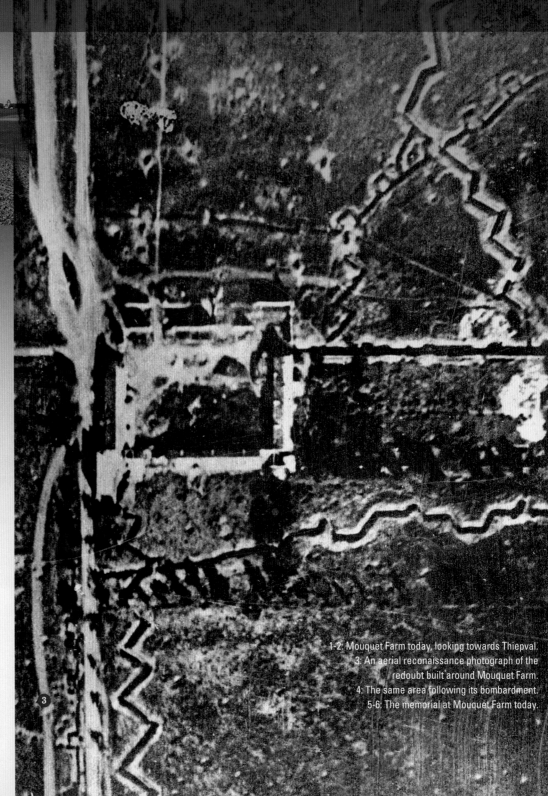

The 1st Australian Division had taken and held the village, except for the OG trenches on its eastern side. On the morning of 25 July the Germans launched a massive counter-attack: 'The enemy came over the ridge like swarms of ants, rushing from shell hole to shell hole. Our men, full of fight and confidence, lined the parapet and emptied magazine after magazine into them. Under this fire and that of our machine-guns and artillery, which tore great gaps in the advancing lines, the enemy attack withered.' **Sergeant H Preston, 9th Australian (Queensland) Bn, 1st Australian Division**.

After this tremendous feat of courage and endurance, the 1st Australian Division was relieved by the 2nd Australian Division. They had sustained 5000 casualties. At quarter past midnight on 29 July the 7th Australian Brigade attacked the OG trenches, where the German defenders were the embodiment of Falkenhayn's defence of every foot of ground. The attack was urged on by Reserve Army Commander Hubert Gough, despite the fact that their preparation was incomplete. Parts of the OG1 trench were taken, but uncut wire along the majority of the attack front caused hundreds of deaths: 'The men dropped like flies, the German wire remained intact and they could go neither forward nor back. They tore at the barbed wire with their hands, searching for openings under one of the most intense machine-gun barrages Australians ever faced.' **Private Tom Young, 27th Australian (South Australia) Battalion, 2nd Australian Division**.

1-2: Mouquet Farm today, looking towards Thiepval.
3: An aerial reconaissance photograph of the redoubt built around Mouquet Farm.
4: The same area following its bombardment.
5-6: The memorial at Mouquet Farm today.

By 3 August the 12th Division was in the line to the left of the Australians, and they launched yet another night attack, this time on the German trenches of Fourth Avenue, north of Pozières towards Mouquet Farm. The attack was successful, with the 8th Royal Fusiliers and 6th Buffs taking almost one hundred prisoners. The next day, 2nd Australian Division again attacked the OG trenches, this time overrunning them, despite meeting strong resistance. The 2nd Australian Division was relieved on 6 August after eventually clearing the rise of Pozières Ridge at the old windmill. The Allies now had sight over Courcelette and Martinpuich, in the direction of Bapaume. And the 2nd Australian Division had lost 6000 men.

The fighting on the ridge towards Mouquet Farm and Thiepval had descended into a nightmare of attrition, with every few yards being bitterly and viciously contested. The barrages of both sides were steadily taking their toll, and more and more Australians were thrown against the stubborn defenders in piecemeal assaults. Hand-to-hand combat in the maze of blown-in trenches were often so confusing that neither side knew who had the upper hand or which bit of cratered, churned up ground they were fighting for. By these means the Allies edged their way closer and closer to Mouquet Farm, the main obstacle to the citadel of Thiepval.

4

5

6

GUILLEMONT

The German Second Position in the south-east of the Somme front ran through the villages of Guillemont and Ginchy down to Maurepas, north of the River Somme. The line ran south past the junction of the British and French armies, and events in this area were often conducted as joint British-French affairs.

Guillemont: the scene of devastation after the barrage and attack showing some of the entrances to the complex tunnel system which formed such an obstacle for the Allies

Strategically, several locations needed to be secured before a general attack upon Guillemont could be launched, including the old sugar refinery at Waterlot Farm. By 17 July, this position had obtained, and a joint British and French attack on the German Second Position was planned for 23 July. A preliminary attack on 20 July by the 35th Bantam Division to achieve better starting positions for the British failed badly – they lost 450 men. On 23 July the 4th Manchester Pals and 2nd Green Howards of 30th Division attacked Guillemont from the direction of Waterlot Farm and Trones Wood. Fighting their way to the east of the village, they were then cut off. By now exhausted, a few of the Manchesters managed to make it back. On 30 July 30th Division attacked again. Maltz Horn Farm was captured, and the 2nd Royal Scots again attacked into the village, taking many prisoners. However, despite receiving support, strong German counter-attacks developed quickly and again, they became cut off. The similarity between the attacks of 23 and 30 July revealed the difficulty attackers faced at Guillemont – the maze of deep underground connecting tunnels meant that once in the village, attackers could quickly be isolated and dealt with.

The forward troops of the 30th and 35th Divisions were brought out of the line after the 30 July attack and replaced with the newly-arrived 55th Division. Their attacks would start on 8 August, in tandem with the 2nd Division. Throughout August, Guillemont became a scene of the most dreadful attrition – and disease. The enormous number of dead out on the battlefields had spawned a plague of fat flies that droned endlessly around the heads of the men as they ate and slept – and as they relieved themselves wherever they could. As a result, many of the men went down with stomach complaints. ▶▶

'The first part of our journey lay through a narrow trench, the floor of which consisted of deep thick mud, and the bodies of dead men trodden underfoot. It was horrible beyond description, but there was no help for it, and on the half rotten corpses of our own brave men we marched in silence, everyone busy with his own thoughts...'

Father William Doyle, Padre, 16th Division

A British soldier killed before even leaving his dugout. His protective breech cover has not been removed from his rifle.

Mortar crews and stretcher-bearers can be seen moving foward in the wake of the front-line troops.

In the heat of summer, constantly agitated by remorseless German shelling, dreadful hygiene and with little opportunity for proper sleep, many of the men had reached a state of desperation. Under these conditions the men of 55th Division made three big attacks on 8, 9 and 12 August. None succeeded, and they lost over 4100 men. The division was relieved in the line at Guillemont by the 24th Division and 3rd Division. The weather broke during the last few days of August, culminating in a terrific thunderstorm in the Somme area on 29 August. By this time, after more fruitless attacks, 3rd Division had been taken out of the line and the Bantams of 35th Division once more found themselves at Guillemont. In front of the village, 24th Division had been replaced by the 20th (Light) Division, and 5th Division were also brought in.

The weather caused several postponements in the joint attack planned with the French, but it was eventually set for 3 September. As the trenches began to dry during the first days of September, morale improved. The British bombardment began at 8am on 2 September. After the exasperation of the previous five weeks, the bombardment was thorough. The village of Guillemont was by now little more than an alien landscape pitted with shell-holes. Trenchlines had disappeared, although deep dugouts were still being used by the defenders. This time, though, the village was overwhelmed, and the 6th Royal Irish advanced to the tune of their battalion pipers. Huge numbers of weary prisoners were taken, greatly relieved that their prolonged defence was over. 700 prisoners were taken, whilst German corpses lay scattered in profusion all around the village.

From 26 August to 7 September, 5th Division's casualties were 4233 officers and men. 20th Division's were 2959 officers and men. The German writer and artist Ernst Jünger served at Guillemont. His account of the battle is told in his "Storm of Steel", published in Germany after the war's end; it remains one of the most remarkable descriptions of the war from the German perspective.

Within eight weeks of the launch of the Allied offensive on the Somme, a change of command was forced upon the Germans. The new commanders understood the need for full mobilization of the economy and civilian population in order to win the war.

HINDENBURG AND LUDENDORFF TAKE OVER

Right: General Erich von Falkenhayn took over effective command of the German Army from Colonel-General Helmuth Graf von Moltke on 14 September 1914. Moltke was kept in position for a further two months to avoid damaging moral. Falkenhayn's experience of traditional military tactics did not give him the experience necessary to handle a immobile war of attrition. He was replaced by Paul von Hindenburg, who was promoted Field Marshal and General Ludendorff. Falkenhayn took command of the Ninth Army on the Eastern Front and then moved to command German forces in Palestine.

Left: Hindenburg, to the left, Ludendorff, to the right explaining their plans to the Kaiser.

The failure of Falkenhayn's strategy on the Western Font precipitated both his removal from office and a huge shift in German strategy. By the end of August General Paul Von Hindenburg was made Chief of the General Staff, with General Erich Ludendorff his deputy. With the arrival of Hindenburg and Ludendorff, the Kaiser lost much of his power to influence the war, and the inherently autocratic structure of German society allowed the new German High Command by turns to assume power at all levels – effectively establishing a military dictatorship. The population and economy were fully mobilized, and the seeds of destruction for the German people which would bear fruit a quarter of a century later had begun to take root.

The attrition being waged on the Somme led Hindenburg and Ludendorff to introduce a radical new policy of 'defence in depth'. They moved away from the concept of holding ground regardless of the cost in troops, and on 23 September 1916 – a little over halfway through the Battle of the Somme – Germany began work on the 'Siegfried Stellung' – which for the British became the Hindenburg Line – almost 20 miles to the rear of their existing front lines.

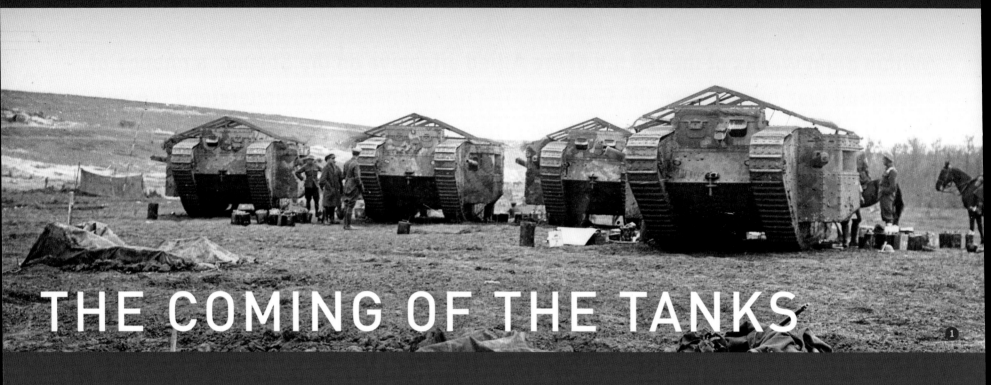

THE COMING OF THE TANKS

The village of Ginchy, like its close neighbour Guillemont, had seen terrible scenes of attritional fighting, but it was eventually captured on 9 September, by the 16th (Irish) Division. The fall of Ginchy cleared the way for Haig and Rawlinson's next big attack, and with intelligence reports indicating the imminent collapse of the German Army on the Somme, Haig again harboured ambitions of a major breakthrough. It was to be a multi-divisional attack on the German Third Position, in conjunction with the French Sixth Army. The British attack was across a wide front that stretched from an area close to Mouquet Farm, through Courcelette and Martinpuich, villages either side of the Albert-Bapaume Road, down to Flers, north of Delville Wood. The French, adjoining the British in the south, were to attack east of Combles.

The 15 September battle marked the introduction into the Somme campaign of Canadian and New Zealand forces, but is chiefly remembered now because it was the first use of the 'tank' in warfare. Two Canadian divisions formed the left of the British line, astride the Albert-Bapaume road at Pozières. To their right were the 15th Scottish, 50th and 47th London Divisions (as we have seen, the 47th Division was to do battle in High Wood). The New Zealand Division was next along the attack front, and beyond them were brigades from 41st and 14th Divisions. The Guards Division and elements from the 6th and 56th Divisions made up the extreme right of the line.

The tank was to make its debut at several locations along this broad attack front. Altogether there were to be 48 of these British secret weapons dramatically entering the attack. The huge element of surprise was a key part of Haig and Rawlinson's strategy here, although it also meant that the pre-attack barrage had to leave gaps so that the tanks would have an easier passage to the German line. The barrage was also

1: Newly arrived tanks being prepared for action. With a speed of around 2mph they were outstripped by the infantry advance and many of them had broken down well before reaching the enemy trenches. They acquired the name 'tank' in an effort to deceive the Germans of their function, being a shorthand for "water-tank".

'A tank is walking up the High Street of Flers with the British Army cheering behind.' English newspaper report

not as intense as that used on 14 July, and consequently some divisions had great difficulty in advancing against unsuppressed enemy fire.

The Guards Division made good progress, although stopping short of their objective of Lesboeufs. On the left of the attack, the Canadians swept through the trenches, taking no prisoners in the ferocious fighting. With the help of a further barrage and the arrival of support troops, they surged onwards through Courcelette, and by the day's end had captured important parts of the Fabeck Graben Trench, thereby isolating Mouquet Farm, south of Thiepval. The Kiwis attacked towards Flers, and overran the Switch Line – an important element of the Germans' defence and one of the reasons that High Wood had withstood so much pressure.

Across much of the attack front, the tanks had not contributed materially to the advance, save for the shock they had caused the defenders when some machines did manage to reach the Germans. Many of them had broken down before reaching the enemy trenches. An exception, famously, was at Flers, where the 41st Division captured the village. Four tanks managed to reach the village, and the progress of one – D16 – subsequently led to a 'colourful account' in the newspapers back home.

By the end of the day, the British had advanced 2500 yards and captured 4500 yards of the German Third Position. It was at a cost though – Fourth Army's casualties were estimated at almost 29,000, and the French casualties were also high – their attack had failed. Furthermore, the Germans had funnelled back to new trenchlines dug to the rear of their Third Position.

Despite all the solid advances, Haig's ambition to break out into open country was again left unfulfilled.

SUCCESS AT MORVAL

A Mark 1 tank moving up to the front under the bemused gaze of the infantry. The tank had a crew of eight and was powered by a 105 horsepower Daimler engine developed to drive tractors. The two guns fitted in the sponsons were naval 6-pounders with shortened barrels. Painted in field camouflage colours the first tanks also had a wooded canopy to protect them from the blast of grenades and shells.

Originally set for 21 September as an attack alongside the French, Fourth Army's attack on Morval was postponed because of the weather to 25 September. The French preferred to attack during the day, so Rawlinson decided not to employ tanks here, instead concentrating on a thunderous 'creeping' bombardment across the entire attack front, which in the event greatly assisted the infantry advance.

The objective was to take what had not been achieved on 15 September and make a limited advance of 1500 yards. The bombardment began on 24 September, and was truly murderous in its intensity – 40 per cent heavier than on 15 September. Without the time now to construct substantial concrete dugouts, the Germans were left without shelter against the bombardment. The infantry attack was consequently highly effective, with individual heroics amidst 5th Division's roaring success as it overran Morval – Private 'Todger' Jones winning his VC by capturing and bringing back over one hundred German prisoners. The Guards and 6th Divisions took Lesboeufs and the New Zealanders also made substantial progress.

The next day, Gird Trench, before Guedecourt, was captured by 21st Division, aided by one of the tanks that had been engaged at Flers, D17. It travelled down the line of the trench directing fire into it, killing a great number of the enemy. 375 prisoners were also taken, for only 5 wounded men. Guedecourt village was taken easily some hours later. The village of Combles, to the south of the attack, was now almost isolated, and the defenders abandoned it. The Germans, rather than standing to the last man, were now using more flexible tactics and falling back to fresh positions when necessary. Overhead, the Royal Flying Corps observed that a new defensive position had been constructed on Le Transloy Ridge.

'With sufficient time to prepare for an assault on a definite and limited objective, I believe that a well-trained division can capture almost any "impregnable" stronghold, and this doctrine has been taught to the 18th Division'

Major General FI Maxse, commander, 18th (Eastern) Division

THE JEWEL IN THE CROWN

With Haig evermore convinced that the German Army was cracking, he ordered hard attacks against objectives that had remained untaken since the slaughter of the first day, and whilst Fourth Army were busy performing heroics at Morval, Gough's Reserve Army was engaged in an attempt to overcome the dogged resistance of German troops along the Thiepval Spur and Schwaben Redoubt areas.

The line had now closed in around Thiepval from the south, and stood before Mouquet Farm. Further round to the west, the German defences had been gradually eroded so that the upper reaches of Blighty Valley were now free of the machine-gun positions that had so devastated the attacks of 32nd and 8th Divisions on 1 July – the Nordwerk had been captured and part of the Leipzig Salient south of Thiepval was now in British hands. Here, the attack was carried to the Germans by Maxse's 18th Division, whilst Mouquet Farm was assaulted by the 11th Northern Division. On their right, the Canadians attacked towards Regina Trench, north of Courcelette.

Above: Stretcher-bearers bring the wounded back from the line.
Right: Exhausted troops snatching some rest in dismal conditions.

The wasteland that was Thiepval

After all the trials that the British Army had suffered since 1 July, the attack on Thiepval was carried forward in a vigorous and determined assault which resulted in very few prisoners being taken. The 12th Middlesex fought its way through to the rubble of Thiepval Château, and by nightfall most of the ruined village had been taken in the most brutal fashion. Throughout the night they were subjected to a terrific counter-barrage. Emerging from this in the daylight of dawn, the shocking sight of decaying dead from 1 July met their eyes: craters and trenches full of corpses, both British and German.

The 7th Bedfords relieved the exhausted troops and went forward to take the remainder of the village on 27 September. Mouquet Farm by this time had also been overrun. A day later, they attacked and took parts of the Schwaben Redoubt, but persistent German counter-attacks prevented them from finally securing it until seven days later. Thereafter, as winter began to extend its grip, the fighting became clogged by the monstrous and ubiquitous mud. Beneath Thiepval, the battle on the Ancre would now be fought out amidst terrible conditions which would soon bring the offensive to a close.

125

Weather conditions on the Ancre meant that cumbersome waterproofs and trench waders had to be worn.

> 'We've got in mind what we got to do. We know we're for the slaughterhouse. We know that the 29th Division, the Newfoundlanders, the Essex and everybody else got slaughtered. We know that!
>
> Ordinary Seaman Joe Murray, Hood Battalion, 63rd (Royal Naval) Division.

THE BATTLE OF THE ANCRE

- 31st Division
- 51st Highland Division
- 63rd Royal Naval Division
- 19th Division
- 39th Division
- 3rd Division
- 2nd Division

By the time the order came for the late push by the River Ancre, most of the men had assumed the battle to be done. By November most of the greenery had disappeared along the front line, and a cratered and blasted wasteland now dominated a huge area. On top of this, the weather was appalling. The summer of 1916 was the wettest of the war, and the sodden ground conditions got worse as the Autumn wore on. The communication trenches were now rivers and quagmires, with troops having to adopt the dangerous option of getting around above ground and, despite the more durable nature of their trenches, the Germans were having almost as much trouble as the British moving around. The wire in front of their trenches was still intact though, just as it had been on 1 July, and clinging to it were what remained of the British dead from that infamous day, mostly decomposed within the remnants of their uniforms. Putrefaction, the flies of summer and the legions of rats had seen to most of the flesh. Since then, the Germans had also reinforced the existing wire.

With another Allies' meeting at Chantilly looming, Haig needed something substantial to bring to the table. If the British could finally take Serre, Beaumont Hamel, Beaucourt and St. Pierre Divion – all of which being original 1 July objectives – before the winter properly set in, ambitious plans for the spring of 1917 could be put in hand. Gough's orders therefore were to prepare his army for an offensive astride the Ancre, running north through Beaumont Hamel and Redan Ridge up to Serre.

The bulk of the attack was to be carried by V Corps, and in the line was the 31st Division, again on the extreme left, although just north of their deployment opposite Serre on 1 July – scene of their bloody undoing. 3rd Division now took the position opposite Serre, and 2nd Division would attack the Redan Ridge. The 51st (Highland) Division would attack down at Beaumont Hamel, with the 63rd Royal Naval Division taking the line down to the Ancre – their objective was the railway station in the village of Beaucourt. Over the river were two divisions of II Corps – the 19th and 39th. The preparations for the attack were thorough, and of necessity included many of the men digging whole new sections of trench and repairing the roads up to the front. The battle was originally planned for 24/25 October, but the continual poor weather meant delays in the start date. It was eventually fixed for 13 November, with the barrage opening on 11 November. ▶▶

At 5.45am on 13 November the attack was announced by a huge explosion in the old Hawthorn Ridge crater of 1 July – blown for a second time. At Beaumont Hamel, 51st (Highland) Division (with the self-deprecatory nickname of 'Harper's Duds') attacked under a creeping barrage, and also the recent innovation of a machine-gun barrage. Tanks were also employed. They succeeded where the 29th Division had failed on 1 July and took the village. On their right, the 63rd Royal Naval Division were also successful in fighting through the German defences, thanks in no small part to the decisive leadership of Colonel Bernard Freyberg. He rallied his men of Hood Battalion onto their objective of Beaucourt Railway Station, winning his VC in the act. Over the Ancre, St. Pierre Divion was captured by the 39th Division, and 19th Division also took their objectives.

Meanwhile, up on Redan Ridge and Serre, progress was not as good. 2nd Division did eventually advance some way into the German lines on Redan Ridge, but the German defences remained steadfast around Serre, and both 3rd and 31st Divisions' attacks failed badly. The German wire remained largely uncut, and in particular, the Hull Pals of 31st Division, who had largely escaped the slaughter of 1 July by being in reserve, sustained heavy casualties. The 12th and 13th East Yorks, the 'Hull Mob' – lost over 800 officers and men, although in the midst of their attack, Private John Cunningham of the 12th East Yorks – the 'Hull Sportsmen' – won the only VC to be awarded in all the fighting at Serre. In 3rd Division's attack there were dreadful losses too. The 2nd Suffolks of 76th Brigade attacked out of the Sheffield and Accrington trenches of 1 July, and with lamentably similar results. Uncut German wire resulted in their attack coming to an abrupt halt, and they suffered horrendous casualties – all told, 533 officers and men. Serre had again taken its toll of the Pals, and it was to remain in German hands for a further three months.

1-3. The low-lying Ancre region then and now, showing how easily the levels on the banks of the river can become flooded.
4. The mill on the Ancre, one of several objectives of the battle.

THE END OF THE BATTLE

'I have never seen such desolation. Mud thin, deep and black, shell holes full of water, corpses all around in every stage of decomposition, some partially devoid of flesh, some swollen and black, some fresh, lying as if in slumber. Our trenches are little more than joined-up shell holes, mostly with twelve inches of water above twelve inches of mud...'

Captain Alfred Bundy, 2nd Middlesex, 8th Division

The waterlogged, pitted and defoliated landscape beside the Ancre by November

After the success of the Battle of Morval, Rawlinson, pushed on by Haig's insistent desire to break through into open country, continued the attack towards Bapaume. With the Fifth Army gearing up for the battle on the Ancre, Fourth Army was to break the new German Transloy Line. Eaucourt L'Abbaye and Le Sars had been taken in the first week of October, but most of the attacks throughout the rest of the month were largely without success. Despite appeals from various quarters on the folly of persisting with these futile attacks, they continued. One such objective was the very conspicuous Butte de Warlencourt, only 500 yards along the Albert-Bapaume road from Le Sars. This was a round barrow, 60 feet high, 'a prehistoric tumulous, standing up like Silbury Hill beside the Bath Road... a dome of gleaming white chalk...', was how Lieutenant Charles Carrington described it. The Germans used the Butte as an observation post, and it commanded views across the shallow valley that the British now controlled. Several attempts were made to take it, but without success. The Civil Service and Post Office Rifles of 47th London Division lost many of their men trying. So did the Durham Light Infantry, who managed to take the trenches around the Butte, but could not hold them. It stayed in German hands until their withdrawal to the Hindenburg Line at the end of February 1917. There was no definitive action to close the Battle of the Somme. The fighting died away as the weather encroached, and surviving the onset of winter became a more pressing concern to both armies.

THE COST

By the Battle's end in November, Britain, France and Germany had lost an enormous number of men, both dead and permanently disabled. The casualty figures were staggering, and in Britain, there were now calls for a compromise peace with Germany. Politicians at all levels were concerned about the permanent impact upon the fabric of the nation that the Battle of the Somme had caused. With no end to the war with Germany in sight, what on earth was going to happen when hostilities resumed in the Spring? For France's part, Joffre was actually critical of the British for 'breaking off the battle too soon' – and claimed that a decisive victory over Germany could have been possible if the British had continued.

In any case, the Official History of 1916 attempts a studied calculation of losses sustained on the Somme by Britain, France and Germany. German casualties are stated as being between 660,000 and 680,000, and total combined British and French casualties 'reckoned at less than 630,000'. On a simple balance-sheet equation, the Allies came out in front. As it was, the British dead amounted to 127,751, which over the course of the Battle from 1 July to 20 November, is a daily average of 893. For this cost, on the Somme front, the British and French had moved the Germans back approximately 7 miles.

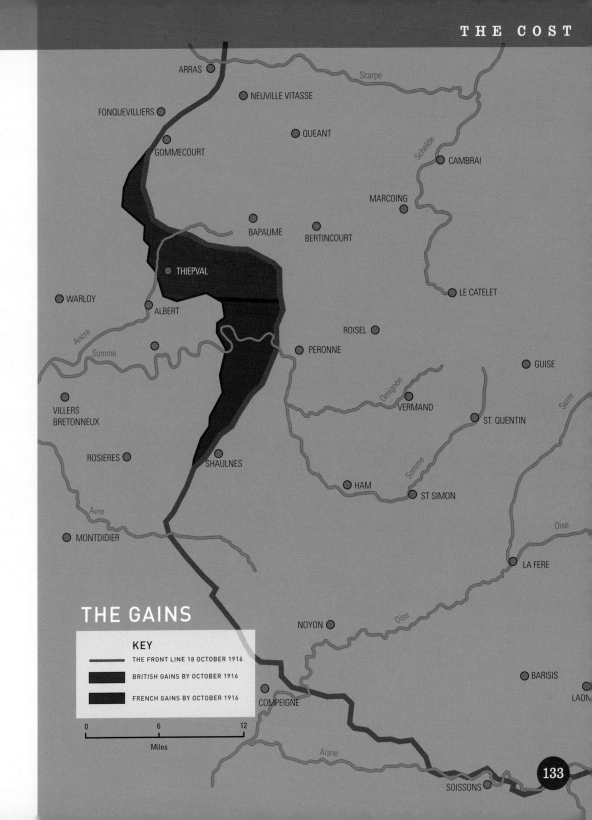

THE GAINS

KEY

— THE FRONT LINE 18 OCTOBER 1916

▮ BRITISH GAINS BY OCTOBER 1916

▮ FRENCH GAINS BY OCTOBER 1916

0   6   12
Miles

133

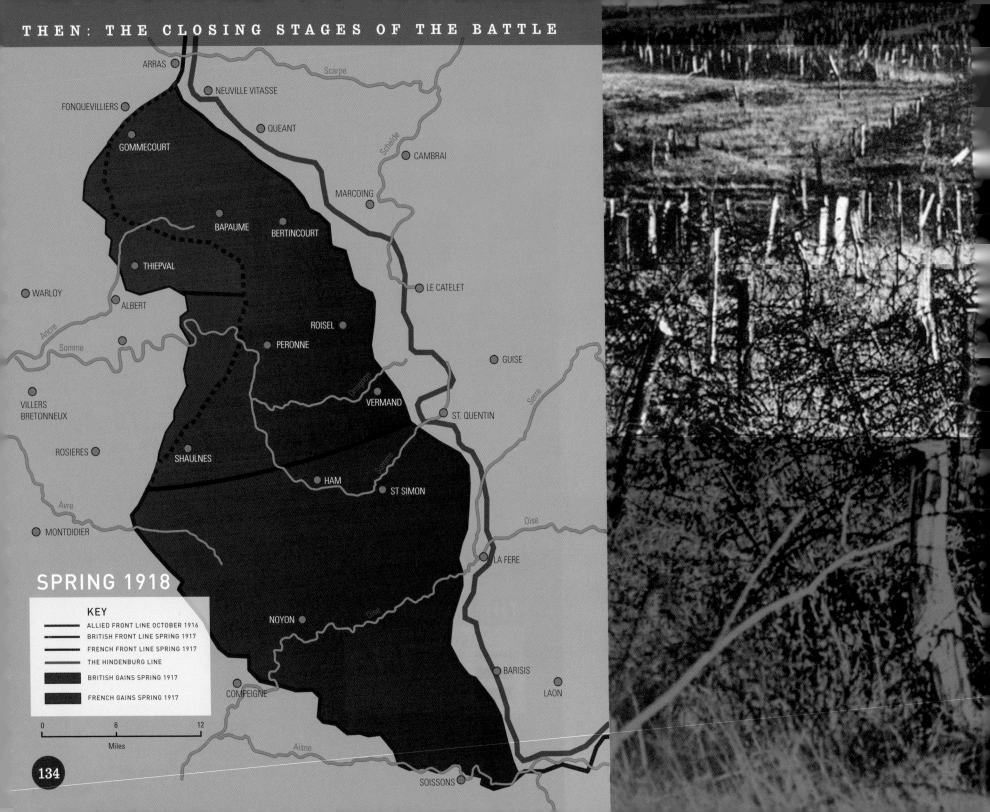

SPRING 1918

KEY

— ALLIED FRONT LINE OCTOBER 1916
— BRITISH FRONT LINE SPRING 1917
— FRENCH FRONT LINE SPRING 1917
— THE HINDENBURG LINE
■ BRITISH GAINS SPRING 1917
■ FRENCH GAINS SPRING 1917

0   6   12
Miles

ARRAS

NEUVILLE VITASSE

FONQUEVILLIERS

QUEANT

GOMMECOURT

CAMBRAI

MARCOING

BAPAUME

BERTINCOURT

THIEPVAL

LE CATELET

WARLOY

ALBERT

ROISEL

PERONNE

GUISE

VILLERS BRETONNEUX

VERMAND

ST. QUENTIN

ROSIERES

SHAULNES

HAM

ST SIMON

MONTDIDIER

LA FERE

NOYON

BARISIS

COMPEIGNE

LAON

SOISSONS

Scarpe

Schelde

Ancre

Somme

Omignon

Somme

Serre

Avre

Oise

Oise

Aisne

THE GERMANS WITHDRAW

'What remained of the old first-class, peace-trained German infantry had been expended on the battlefield.' Crown Prince Rupprecht of Bavaria

In late February 1917 the Germans abandoned all their positions on the Somme and pulled back around 20 miles to their newly fortified position on the Hindenburg Line, carrying out a systematic destruction of the land, towns and villages as they did so. As intended, this withdrawal gave them many tactical advantages but, as Ludendorff admitted, 'The Army had been fought to a standstill and was utterly worn out.' By the end of the Verdun campaign, the French had regained almost all of the ground they had lost, and Captain von Hentig of the Guard Reserve Division famously described the Somme as the 'muddy grave of the German Army.'

135

The 'Old hun line', the Accrington Pals reach the village of Serre in March 1917.

The ruined Hotel de Ville at Péronne, March 1917. Like most front line towns and villages, little was left standing; another untold cost of the war was that of reconstruction.

As Winter 1916-17 set in, both sides were counting their costs and considering their strategies for the next year of campaigning. The British initiative to open a third front in southeastern Europe in 1915, by coordinating with the Russians to drive a wedge between the Ottomans and the southern Austrian border, had foundered at Gallipoli, where Commonwealth troops had sustained heavy losses. However, Italy's entry to the war in the same year had opened a battle front much closer to the Austrian heartland across the Alps.

On the Eastern Front, the Central Powers had made substantial gains, effectively occupying most of former Poland, and reaching the Gulf of Riga; by now they had taken over two million Russian prisoners and, despite the initially successful Brusilov offensives on the southern sector in 1916, the Russian Army was beset by supply shortages, mutinies and war-weariness.

The indecisive naval battle of Jutland in May/June 1916 succeeded in crushing any German hopes for her

Crown Prince Rupprecht of Bavaria. He was to opposed to Ludendorff's 'scorched earth' policy during the German withdrawal to the Hindenburg Line.

A German U-Boat torpedoes a British merchant ship. The U-Boat campaign destroyed over 3.8 million tons of Allied and neutral shipping between February and June 1917.

The arrival of US troops – the 'Doughboys' – on European soil.

navy breaking the Allied maritime blockade. However, the unrestricted U-Boat campaign in the Atlantic against Allied and neutral merchant shipping, which reached a high point in Spring 1917 when over 800,000 tons of shipping was sunk in April, had an unwanted outcome, being one of the factors which provoked the USA into eventually joining the Allied cause in the same month. Although the problems of mobilization, training and transport meant that the effect of this was not immediate, the advent of the Americans would add great weight to the Allied cause.

USA enlistment posters. The limited success of the volunteer campaign in the States led to the Government passing the Selective Service Act of 18 May 1917, ensuring the registration of 11 million men. 4 million men in the USA were actually called up.

Women workers in a munitions plant in Nottingham. Feeding the war machine was critical – British artillery at Passchendaele were firing up to 500,000 shells a day.

Stretcher-bearers struggling through the mud in Autumn 1917. The heavy rains became another major obstacle which limited Allied success.

With the German tactical withdrawal to the heavily-fortified Hindenburg Line in February 1917, long-term Allied strategy had to be reviewed as they moved forward over the hard-fought battlefields of the previous year, now apparently handed to them for free. Both the French and English still focused on the need for a break-through. Capitalizing on the retreat of the Germans, the new French commander-in-chief, Nivelle, devised a strategy for what he considered to be a way of achieving this. It entailed a series of massive offensives at separate points along the front from east of Rheims in the south to Arras in the north, the latter being in the British sector.

The obsession with breakthough ignored the fact that the German withdrawal was designed to shorten their front and build defence in depth, the better to withstand any further Allied offensives. Nivelle's offensive met with mixed fortunes, despite early successes such as the Canadian victory at Vimy Ridge. The strategic objectives of the plan were not reached, again at heavy cost in terms of casualties, but also provoking several mutinies among the French troops. Nivelle was replaced by the defender of Verdun, General Petain, in May, but by then the weight of the war was shifting from French to British shoulders. In June, British troops achieved

A British Mark IV tank stuck in a captured German trench near Cambrai, November 1917

a successful attack at Messines, but were halted by the third battle of Ypres, known as Passchendaele. The bad weather turned the campaign into a muddy quagmire, into which more and more troops were sent in an effort to free the Belgian coast of the Germans. Whilst the casualties sustained by the Allies were high, psychologically the Germans were taken aback by the massive use of artillery and tanks at the battle of Cambrai in late November, despite the fact that they were the victors.

Decorated British 'dud' shells, fired in Flanders. The Germans painted them in patriotic designs with the words "Greetings from Flanders".

Sustaining and resisting war on an industrial scale by now had had a considerable impact on the civilian populations on all home fronts. In Germany, popular support for the war was declining as shortages of food and other essentials had their effect, resulting in widespread food riots, while in France, despite the winding down of German operations around Verdun, the long campaign had partly achieved its aim: to 'bleed France dry'. The living conditions for the soldiers, and sheer scale of losses on both sides, was beginning to become apparent to the populace in general, despite careful filtering of information by censors. However, with women entering the workforce to maintain

output of weapons and supplies, opportunities for sexual equality and political suffrage appeared to be potential incidental benefits from the war. In Russia, there was even a volunteer female armed unit, the Women's Death Battalion, formed in July 1917.

Russian troops returning from the front, many fully supporting the new Bolshevik government. Soon however, civil war would erupt, with the so-called White Russians supported by the western Allies (and after the Armistice, German forces), which saw former comrades pitted against one another for the next three years.

Dissatisfaction with the war afforded an opportunist political dimension in various places, not least with the Arab revolt against Ottoman rule in Arabia, coordinated in part by the British Colonel TE Lawrence. On the Allied side, Irish Republicans mounted the six-day Easter Rising in Dublin in 1916, swiftly suppressed by the 5000 British troops based on the island.

On a far grander scale was the mutinous collapse of the Russian Army, and the February Revolution (in March by the modern calendar) which forced the Tsar to abdicate. The politically reformist Provisional Government which ensued, still supported the war,

but communist soviets sprang up throughout the country, in factories and within the armed forces, forming a radical power base which led to the Bolshevik Revolution in October (November) 1917. The Bolsheviks immediately sued for peace, leading to the Treaty of Brest-Litovsk in December, which ceded most of Belorussia and Ukraine to the Central Powers.

With pressure relieved on the Eastern Front, Germany could focus her strengths on an offensive designed to defeat British and French forces before the Americans could muster in strength. Ludendorff's plan, Operation Michael, made full use of the 80

divisions made available from the East, the divisions already posted in the West, and some specialist, elite offensive troops. He also assembled a mass of artillery to fire both gas and explosives.

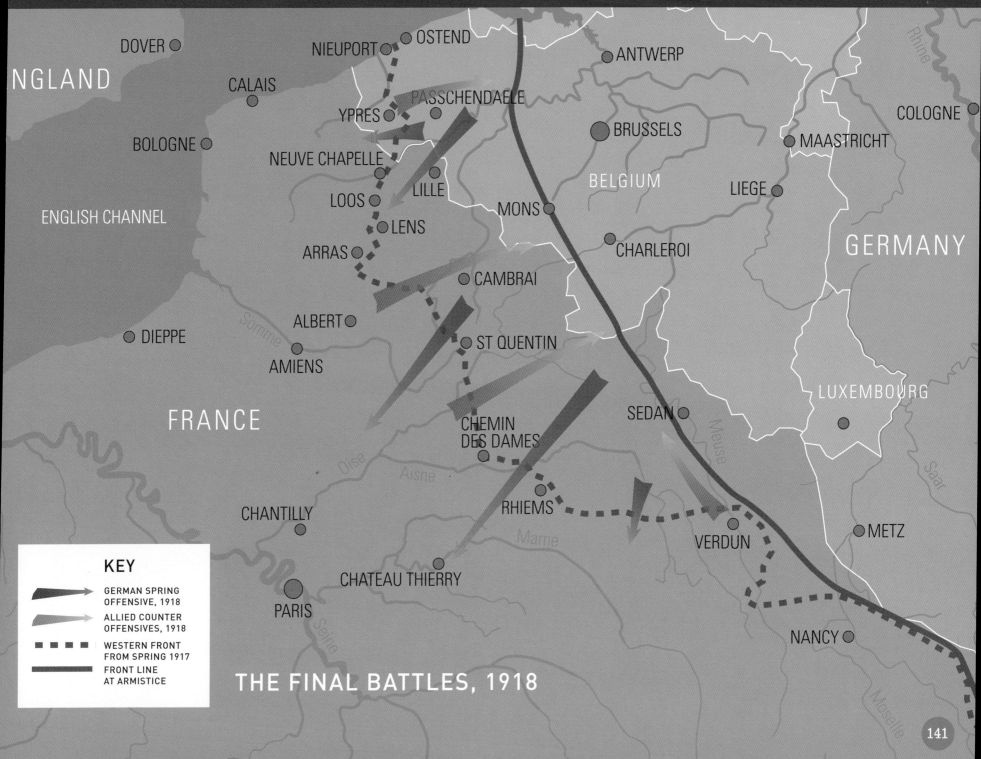

DOVER

NGLAND

CALAIS

BOLOGNE

ENGLISH CHANNEL

DIEPPE

FRANCE

CHANTILLY

PARIS

NIEUPORT

OSTEND

ANTWERP

YPRES

PASSCHENDAELE

BRUSSELS

MAASTRICHT

COLOGNE

NEUVE CHAPELLE

BELGIUM

LIEGE

LILLE

LOOS

MONS

LENS

CHARLEROI

GERMANY

ARRAS

CAMBRAI

ALBERT

Somme

ST QUENTIN

AMIENS

LUXEMBOURG

Oise

Aisne

CHEMIN
DES DAMES

SEDAN

Meuse

Rhine

Saar

RHIEMS

Marne

VERDUN

METZ

CHATEAU THIERRY

Seine

NANCY

Moselle

KEY

GERMAN SPRING
OFFENSIVE, 1918

ALLIED COUNTER
OFFENSIVES, 1918

WESTERN FRONT
FROM SPRING 1917

FRONT LINE
AT ARMISTICE

THE FINAL BATTLES, 1918

141

Germans cross the Chemin des Dames

German attack by an elite commando force, March 1918.

The objectives of the 1918 Spring Offensive were to destroy the British Third and Fifth armies positioned in the Arras and Somme sectors respectively, splitting the French and British by forcing them to shield the Channel ports and Paris respectively, and breaking the Western Front. It was a bold gamble, but the Spring campaign was effectively Germany's last playable card.

Three separate offensives smashed through the front line in the Somme region (March-April), in Flanders (April) on the Aisne (May-June), all gaining substantial ground, reaching Ypres, Mondidier and Château Thierry and regaining more ground than they had ceded the previous year. Two further offensives were mounted, one to consolidate their gains on the Somme and the Aisne (June), and one in the Champagne region between Rheims and Verdun.

Towards the end of the war, weaponry designed for close-quarter fighting, such as this submachine gun, was being developed by both sides.

A dead German soldier, Hamel, March 1918.

'…on the evening of 20 March…I was entirely by myself, and was trying to face up to what I knew was going to be a very unpleasant morning, and probably my last.'

Lieutenant Cyril Dennys, 212 Siege Battery, Royal Guards Artillery

The German view of Villers Bretonneux

A German A7V tank of the sort that fought in the first-ever
tank-to-tank action in April at Cachy, Villers Bretonneux.

In the north, The Third Army repelled the offensive,
whilst the Fifth was overrun, and were it not for the
work of the Australians and the British 18th Division,
particularly at Villers Bretonneux, the Germans may
well have progressed beyond Amiens.

The British appealed to have the French commander-
in-chief, Petain, replaced, and Foch was appointed
on 26 March. This was a key decision as, despite
subordinating the British Army to his command, this
in fact afforded the British Army the opportunity to
display its capabilities, especially its development of
the 'all-arms' offensive.

A Renault FT 17 tank. It was the most successful French tank
of the war, and was also used by the American forces.

29th Australian battalion on 8 August

During the summer months, the Germans continued their relentless attacks on Lys, Champagne and Metz. However, a French counterattack on the Marne on 18 July, spearheaded by the Tenth Army, several hundred Renault tanks and two American divisions dealt a devastating blow to the Germans, resulting in them postponing the offensive and abandoning Soissons. The fact was that despite German hopes and gains, they were now facing overwhelmingly superior manpower and resources. It would only be a matter of time before the longed-for breakthrough would occur.

'…by Jove, the war's coming to an end, we're getting through.'

Private James Southey, Australian Corps

American 33rd Division resting at Corbie, the
day before they joined the Australians.

In the north, an even more devastating blow was struck on 8 August, where in the countryside east of Amiens a combined operation on a massive scale employed huge numbers of Canadian, Australian and British forces, all of whom proved themselves capable of defeating German troops in entrenched positions. It represented the first fully coordinated use of infantry, artillery, armour and air power, and demonstrated the full potential of new weapons and successful communications. The official German version of this campaign, mounted by the French, British and Canadians read: 'As the sun set on 8 August on the battlefield the greatest defeat which

the German Army had suffered since the beginning of the war was an accomplished fact'. By September the Germans had been steadily forced back onto, indeed in places behind, the Hindenburg Line.

The Allies' successful progress continued south with the capture of Péronne. With the capture of land and the recapture of railway lines, ammunition was able to be moved quickly, so that offensives could be launched along all the fronts of the lines.

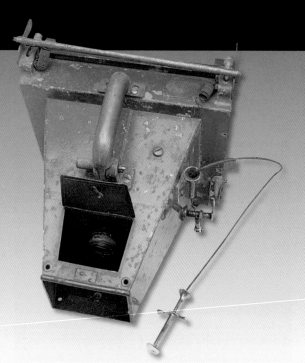

Aerial camera, crucial in gathering the intelligence
required for the planning of the 'all-arms' offensive

Canadian artillery during the battle of Amiens, 10 August.

In late September, a three-pronged offensive was launched, using the American Expeditionary Force under General Pershing, to push up in the south from Verdun through the Argonne Forest; the exhausted French Army was tasked to hold the central section from Champagne to the Somme; Haig's forces mounted a major advance on the sector between St Quentin and Neuve Chapelle, while the regrouped Belgian Army pressed forward through Flanders to regain the eastern region of their nation.

The Germans were steadily pushed back onto the Sambre and Schelde rivers, retreating in increasing disarray as the Allies captured sectors of railway lines essential to their withdrawal.

'...the breakthrough had come. It was open warfare, we were in green fields once again.'

Sergeant-Major Richard, Naval Division

Troops celebrating their victory on the
Riqueval Bridge over the St Quentin canal.

Some of the enormous number of German
prisoners taken after the breaking of the
Hindenburg Line in September.

Right: Crowds on a Paris boulevard celebrate
the Armistice, 11 November 1918.

In April the Germans had been within 40 miles of Paris, and now they had lost hundreds of square miles of territory that they had dominated for over four years, territory that was soaked in the blood of their own troops and their adversaries. How had this happened? The build-up of fresh American troops had been effected more rapidly than the Germans had anticipated – over 300,000 were in France by July, and over one million by November. The British Army were spearheading an Allied force that was now irresistible. But other factors were in play. In southeastern Europe, Germany's Bulgarian allies had surrendered, leaving Austria exposed on its eastern flank, while Italy had gained the upper hand on its very borders. The Ottoman Turks were in retreat in Palestine, and at heart Germany's soldiers, sailors and citizenry were demoralized – mutinies and more rioting was occurring throughout the Fatherland, and troops were refusing to fight or deserting en masse.

By November the Germans, fearful of seeing foreign troops on home soil, were left with little option but to sue for peace, and on 11 November the Armistice was concluded. The guns fell silent, and the 'War to End All Wars' was ostensibly over.

AFTERMATH

Ethical concepts such as Pacifism and Conscientious Objection gained credence during the Great War, as did the medical recognition of the psychological realities of trauma and 'shell-shock'.

The Great War would change the world irreversibly, partly due to the way it was conducted, and partly in the way it affected people and society. The imperially-oriented nations which entered the war were either left in ruins (Austria, Ottoman Turkey), were destroyed only to be rebuilt from within (Russia), or effectively emasculated (Great Britain and France – though the process of dismantling these entities would last for a further half-century). The war's global nature was also to see the birth of an international arbitration and security forum in the League of Nations – forerunner of the United Nations.

But political changes ushered in by the Armistice were to have much more far-reaching and unforeseen consequences. In Germany, the Kaiser was deposed and allowed to retire to Holland, while a republican government initially based in Weimar was installed. The Allies, keen to recover the astronomic costs and losses of the conflict, and to punish the aggressor, imposed crippling penalties on the vanquished in the form of a schedule of 'reparation' payments demanded from Germany. Over the next decade the German economy would be brought to its knees. France reclaimed Alsace-Lorraine, and occupied the German industrial heartland of the Ruhr. Meanwhile a string

of new states were created through Central Europe from the Arctic to the Adriatic – Finland, the Baltic States, a reborn Poland, Czechoslovakia, Austria, Hungary and Yugoslavia appeared on the map, partly to appease nationalist aspirations and partly as a buffer zone to inhibit a rebirth of European imperialism. Strangely, these measures soon had the opposite effect, with popular nationalist/imperialist right-wing dictatorships emerging in Italy, Germany and Spain. Indeed many have ascribed the rise of Nazism (and many of its leaders were Great War veterans) directly to the impact of the Allied treatment of Germany and its citizens in the post-war years, and some propose the view that the First World War was merely the opening phase of the Second.

Industrialization, which had in part been responsible for the war's outbreak, became intrinsic to its conduct, and changed the nature of warfare forthwith. For the first time a war had been fought with the intention of utterly destroying not only the protagonists' armed forces, but their economies and societies as well. While innovative industrial infrastructure and mass-manufacturing techniques underpinned and sustained the war effort on all fronts, and remained critical to the participants' success, new technologies also introduced new ethics. The use of gas, strategic bombing and the unrestricted U-Boat campaign are outstanding examples of this; but paramount in all this was the view taken of front line troops as literally numbers, numbers to be thrown into the turmoil in what became effectively a war of statistics. It is interesting to note that this shift was to produce a situation a quarter of a century later where, in the Second World War, casualties among fighting troops were comparatively much lower, and were far outstripped by the civilian toll.

The social and cultural impacts were equally dramatic. Few families and no communities emerged from the War unscathed or without loss of brothers, fathers, neighbours and comrades. On the other hand, the process of reconstruction proceeded apace, economies were rebuilt, accompanied by improvements in social welfare and, significantly, an acknowledgement of women's new role in society in the form of political suffrage. The reaction to the War's end was one initially of relief, followed by euphoria. Until the Wall Street Crash and the consequent Great Depression changed everything, there was a period of recklessness embodied by the 'Jazz Age'. The trauma of the War introduced a new and intense subjectivity and sense

of dissolution in the arts: the popularity of jazz itself is an obvious example of this, but in painting, abstraction, violence and nihilism found expression in Vorticism, Futurism, the Dada movement (which questioned the very relevance of traditional art), its offspring Surrealism, and, in Revolutionary Russia, Constructivism. In Germany, Expressionism found a new direction, while the Neue Sachlikeit movement reflected the decadent, doomed atmosphere of the Weimar Republic.

The Augustan poets, such as Rupert Brooke, had entered the War with a mere sense of melancholy, while the outstanding 'voices' of the War – the poets such as Wilfred Owen, Siegfried Sassoon, and novelists such as Robert Graves, Edmund Blunden, Richard Aldington, Henri Barbusse and Ernst Jünger spoke with a freshness, directness and honesty which greatly influenced mainstream literature. Interestingly, many of their works were not published until a decade after the war – reliving the immediate past was too painful; RC Sheriff's play 'Journey's End' was first performed in 1928, created a sensation, and opened the way to publication for these poems and memoirs. Sassoon's three novels comprising 'The Memoirs of George Sherston' are most notable in straddling pre-

War culture ('Fox-Hunting Man'), the experience of the trenches ('Infantry Officer'), and the aftermath of shell-shock and disillusion ('Sherston's Progress').

The reclamation of the Great War and its consequences required the passage of time to achieve an historical perspective, conveniently provided by the 50-year embargo on releasing official documents (in Britain at least); thus new scholarship and analyses emerged from the mid-1960s, and influenced the production of the ground-breaking BBC television series 'The Great War'. This process of reclamation has placed the War as a pillar of Britain's cultural heritage for those whose grandfathers and great-grandfathers fought in the trenches, reflected not only in its central position on the national history curriculum in many countries, but in the popularity of treatments ranging from books like Faulkes' 'Birdsong' and Pat Barker's 'Regeneration Trilogy' to BBC's 'Blackadder Goes Forth'.

THE SOMME TODAY

Unlike Verdun, where much of the battlefield has been preserved as a French national memorial, the fields of the Somme have been largely reclaimed by farmers and other local businesses, many of the flattened villages rebuilt, and in many ways the scars of the battle wiped from the landscape. Nevertheless, there are hundreds of memorials and cemeteries scattered across the region.

The Somme is deeply entrenched in our culture. It is a hugely iconic event that exerts a haunting fascination upon each successive generation. Interest in the Great War was rekindled during the 1960s when, because of the 50 Year Rule, information began to be released by the Government that added much information about this tormented period of our history. Since its publication in 1971, Martin Middlebrook's groundbreaking study "First Day on the Somme" has fired the imaginations of historians and everyday readers alike.

Today the region is visited in increasing numbers by historians, schoolchildren, battlefield tourists, genealogists, the military – and the merely curious. A service industry has grown up around this interest, one whose origins can be traced to the aftermath of the War. There are almost 250 British cemeteries on the Somme, with over 100 memorials to Divisions, Pals Battalions and individuals who fought and died at particular locations along the line, from 1 July through to the battle's close on 18 November. All of them honour the sacrifice and deeds of courage performed amidst the horrors of the Somme.

IN MEMORIAM

AT THE GOING DOWN OF THE SUN

1. The Mill Road Cemetery by the Ulster Tower.
2. French students in Connaught Cemetery, where many of the 36th Ulsters, and more than 1200 soldiers of the Royal Naval Division are buried.
Previous pages: Queen's Cemetery at Serre, looking up the hill towards the old German front line, from the entrance to Sheffield Memorial Park. The remains of the jumping-off trenches from 1 July are still visible, running along the edge of the park.

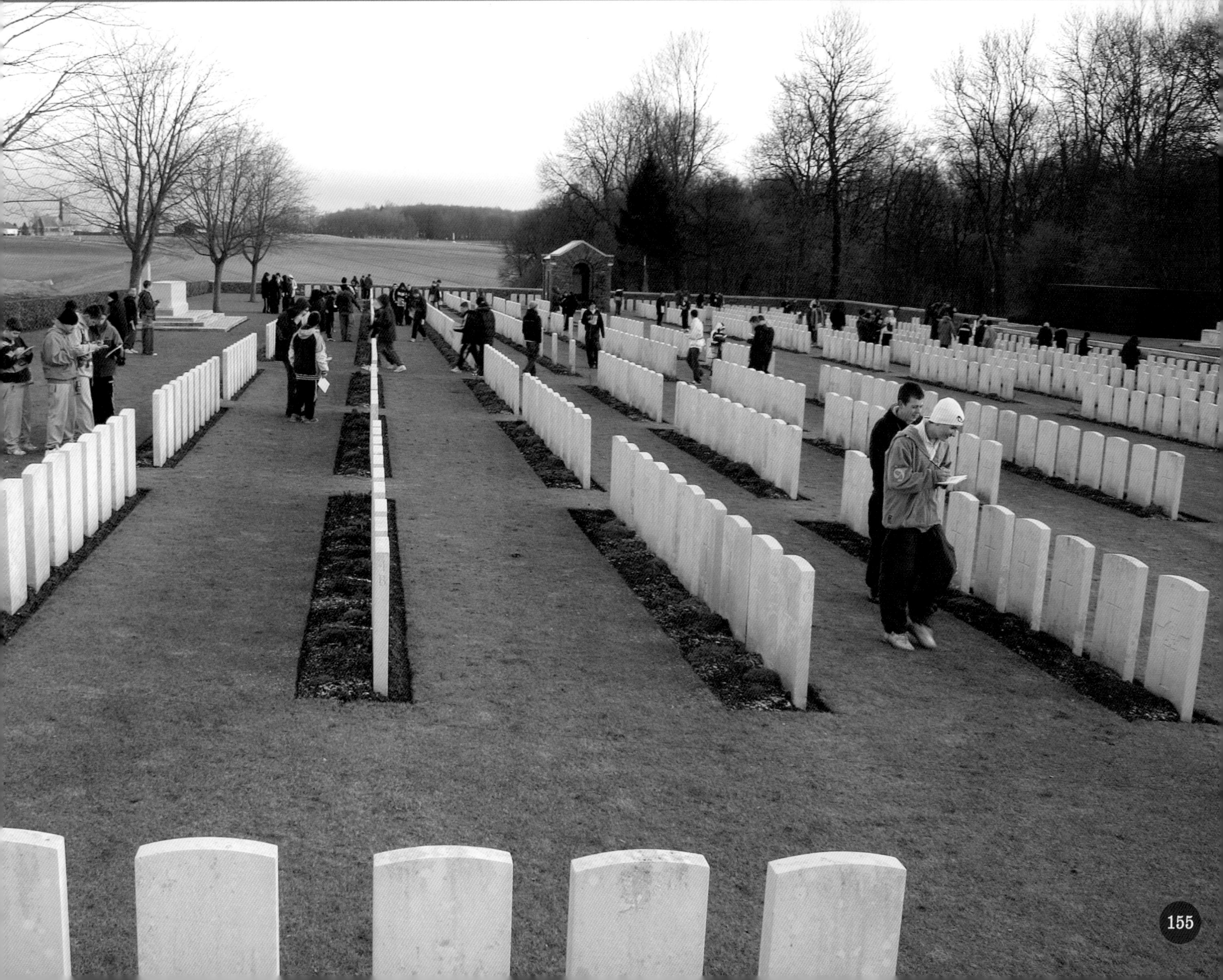

Early on in the conflict, the grim task of registering soldiers graves was undertaken by a Red Cross unit led by Fabian Ware. In recognition of his ceaseless devotion to duty, in 1915 it officially became known as the Graves Registration Commission. Such became the extent of its activities, and such became its importance, particularly following the losses on the Somme, that in 1917 it was conferred a Royal Charter, and thus became the Imperial War Graves Commission (IWGC).

The IWGC was responsible for the appointment of the architects and teams of assistant architects to create worthy cemeteries and memorials.

After the Armistice, the IWGC set about constructing a headquarters on the Somme. It consisted of no more than a collection of huts by the side of the Albert-Bapaume road, but it became a focal point for the tradesmen that gathered there to undertake the task of creating the cemeteries, including the architects, stone masons, carpenters and landscape gardeners.

Much of the workforce were ex-servicemen who willingly undertook the often harrowing task of re-interring their former comrades-in-arms.

After the Second World War, the role of the commission increased dramatically, responding to the aftermath of a truly global conflict, and in 1960, the IWGC was renamed the Commonwealth War Graves Commission.

With its charter to commemorate in perpetuity the brave men and women who died for the cause of freedom and the protection of their homelands, the CWGC continues to this day to build and maintain sites throughout the world.

1. Fabian Ware, founder of the Imperial War Graves Commission.
2. King George V, General Sir Douglas Haig and Fabian Ware visiting a Western Front cemetery.
3. The grisly work of disinterring former comrades.

FABIAN WARE AND THE IMPERIAL WAR GRAVES COMMISSION

As there was to be no repatriation of the soldiers who died, it was agreed that they should be commemorated where they fell in action. Moreover, the Imperial War Graves Commission made the decision that the graves of all the men should be treated identically, with no distinction being made between officers and men – a continuation of the 'brotherhood of the trenches' that had existed during the war, .

The IWGC appointed three architects – Sir Edwin Lutyens, Reginald Blomfield (who also specialized in landscape gardening), and the South African Herbert Baker. They were charged with the task of creating the cemeteries and memorials with a coherent style and dignity. Experts from the Royal Botanical Gardens at Kew also contributed. Teams of assistants helped the architects to carry through the massive programme on a short time-scale.

The cemeteries varied considerably in size. In some cases it became more practical to create larger cemeteries, in which men from the surrounding area were brought together, such as Serre Road No 2. The author Rudyard Kipling, whose son was killed in action, was moved to remark that the architects had been responsible for creating what he termed the 'Silent Cities'.

Notable features of the cemeteries were the Great War Stone designed by Lutyens, and the Cross of Sacrifice designed by Blomfield. Gradually, the makeshift crosses were replaced with simple, dignified headstones in Portland stone. During the two year delay imposed on the enterprize by the Treasury (a reminder of the continuing cost of the war), there was much public and parliamentary debate regarding what inscriptions ought be allowed on the headstones.

1. One of the original battlefield cemeteries.
2. Fabian Ware with other members of IWGC as construction began.
3. The immaculately tended grounds at Fricourt New Military Cemetery.

THE BATTLEFIELD CEMETERIES

THE PILGRIMS

During the 1920s, relatives of the missing, seeking to discover where their loved ones had fallen, undertook the often arduous journey by road, sea, rail and farmtrack, to the battlefields and burial grounds of France.

Lasting for days, the journey for these pilgrims almost invariably ended at a desolate muddy track. As a government initiative, the result of lengthy pressure and lobbying, funding was made available and the enterprize gained steady popularity; often whole communities would travel *en masse* to France.

These pilgrims, usually dressed in formal mourning attire, were a pitiful sight on the old battlefields, searching for a single cross with a name on it among the thousands that confronted them. For the first time they could gain some idea of the reality of war for themselves, and experience the often horrific world in which their loved ones fought and fell. For many, sustained on the Home Front by propaganda and censored letters, this came as a terrible shock.

British governmental support for the surviving wives and children, was promoted by Haig, and became one of the foundations of the charter of the Royal British Legion: to arrange for, and assist them in visiting the graves of relatives killed in war. These tours started in 1927, once the memorials and cemeteries were largely in place. In the first year they took 150 pilgrims to the Western Front, but by 1928 this number had mushroomed to 10,000.

Today, under the auspices of the Royal British Legion, Remembrance Travel continues to provide the same service, and indeed with a wider remit to include all-comers.

1. Crowds of pilgrims arriving at the cemeteries.
2. The Michelin tyre and travel publishing company began to publish detailed tourist guides to the battlefields of the Western Front in 1919.
3, 4. Visitors often had to search for hours among the serried ranks of wooden crosses to identify the one they had travelled so far to find.

4

TO
OUR GLORIOUS DEAD

1914-1918

MEMORIALS AT HOME

1. The memorial at Streatham.
2. The Cenotaph in Whitehall, focal point of British Remembrance. Constructed in plaster and wood as a temporary structure for the first Remembrance Day in 1919, a permanent version was subsequently put in place.
3. The Barnsley memorial.
4. The Royal Artillery memorial at Hyde Park Corner. It is said that the stone howitzer points towards the Somme.

The scale and number of commemorative monuments throughout Great Britain reflects the impact of the war on each and every community. The awful loss of life during the conflict was compounded for the communities back home by the fact that there was to be no repatriation of the dead. Architecture and sculpture therefore played a large part in giving form to this collective grief, with memorials often sited in the very heart of villages, towns and cities. There are over 60,000 of these familiar features across the length and breadth of the country.

Both public and private funding created an array of memorials and monuments that ranged from simple plaques to stained-glass windows, village halls and clock towers. In some universities and schools, cloisters and chapels were built, and in some cases, whole buildings – such as the Birmingham Hall of Memory. In some towns, memorial hospitals and parks were established.

The most important and widely revered of all these constructions is the Cenotaph, designed by Sir Edwin Lutyens. It stands solemn and elegant amidst the traffic of Whitehall, by the Foreign Office and within site of the Houses of Parliament. Every year our national Service of Remembrance takes place here. The Tomb of the Unknown Soldier is in nearby Westminster Abbey. The French equivalent lies beneath the Arc de Triomphe in Paris.

163

THE MEMORIAL TO THE MISSING OF THE SOMME

THIEPVAL

Standing on one of the highest points of the Somme battlefield is the massive, brooding, Memorial to the Missing of the Somme. Designed by Sir Edwin Lutyens, it is the largest British war memorial, and his towering masterpiece. Its aura reaches out for many miles across the surrounding killing fields.

Its sheer size is commensurate with what it commemorates, for around its 16 piers are inscribed the names of some 72,000 men – the Missing of the Somme of 1916. They are the men of Britain and her Commonwealth and dominions who fought and died on the Somme and whose bodies were never found.

Commencing in 1928, it took four years to construct, and was inaugurated by HRH The Prince of Wales and the French Premier Albert Lebrun in 1932.

Originally, the Memorial held over 73,000 names, but since 1932 the remains of around 1000 of the Missing have been discovered and identified. On the occasions that this has happened, the remains are formally interred with military honours and their names removed from engraved list. Beneath the void of its enormous arch, is the Great War Stone which states 'Their Name Liveth For Evermore'.

1. The Prince of Wales with Major-General Sir Fabian Ware at the inauguration of the Memorial to the Missing at Thiepval. Lutyens can be seen in the background of the picture, to the left.
2. Building the Thiepval memorial.

165

MEMORY AND REMEMBRANCE NOW

At precisely 7.28 am on 1 July every year at La Boisselle, an explosion simulates the blowing of the mine at the site which became known as the Lochnagar Crater. To the throng of whistles blown by the pilgrims standing at the crater's edge, a lone piper emerges from the smoke traces of the explosion, and heralds the beginning of a moving service to the memory of the men that fell during the battle of the Somme in 1916.

1 July has continued to be commemorated every year since the Armistice. In Salford the day used to be known as Thiepval Day, in recognition of the men of the area who lost their lives there. Their colours were placed in Salford's Trinity Church, perhaps something of an oversight, as most of the Salford Pals were first or second generation Irish Roman Catholic, brought over to help build the Manchester Ship Canal.

Throughout the day there are a number of public services along the 1 July front of 1916, including Thiepval, the Ulster Tower, and Beaumont Hamel. These are often attended by Royalty, politicians, soldiers, veterans, civic dignitaries, pilgrims and military history enthusiasts. In some corners of the battlefield, small and more intimate services also take place.

The more widely observed national Festival of Remembrance in the United Kingdom is marked by a two-minutes' silence on the Eleventh hour of the Eleventh day of 11 November – the moment when the Armistice was signed and the guns fell silent across Europe.

The function of remembrance is not confined to services, relatives, descendants, servicemen and women. Study of the Great War is included on the national school curricula in Britain, where a special focus is placed on the Battle of the Somme, as well as in France, and in Germany. Over a quarter of a million visitors pass through the various Western Front visitor centres every year - a large proportion of them schoolchildren.

1. 1 July Memorial Service at Thiepval, 2005.
2. The Thiepval Memorial today.

2

1

IN FLANDERS' FIELDS
JOHN MCCRAE, 1915

THE ROYAL BRITISH LEGION

In Flanders' fields the poppies blow
Between the crosses, row on row,
That mark our place: and in the sky
The larks, still bravely singing, fly
Scarce heard amid the guns below.

We are the dead. Short days ago
We lived, felt dawn, saw sunset glow,
Loved and were loved, and now we lie
In Flanders' fields.

Take up our quarrel with the foe:
To you from failing hands we throw
The torch; be yours to hold it high,
If ye break faith with us who die
We shall not sleep, though poppies grow
In Flanders' Fields.

The poppy is the symbol of the Royal British Legion but the idea originated in America. An American War Secretary, Moina Michael, inspired by John McCrae's poem, began selling poppies to friends to raise money for the ex-service community. And so the tradition began.

The Royal British Legion is the UK's leading charity providers of financial, social and emotional support to millions who have served and are currently serving in the Armed Forces, and their dependents. Today, nearly 10.5 million people are eligible for their support and they receive thousands of calls for help every year. The Legion was founded in 1921 as a voice for the ex-service community and over 450,000 members continue to ensure that this voice does not go unheard. Although the needs of ex-servicemen and women have changed over the years, they are still there to safeguard their welfare, interests and memory.

The most high profile fundraising event undertaken by the Legion is the annual Service of Remembrance, attended by the Royal Family, politicians and ex-servicemen and women, during which the two minutes' silence is observed. The event is preceded by the annual Poppy Appeal. But the Legion undertakes more than just financial relief. It also provides convalescent homes and respite facilities for ex-service personnel, and is an active and strong campaigning voice for many ex-service issues.

British service people are in action around the world every day of the year. They know that if they need the support of the Legion – now or in the future – the Legion is always on active duty for them.

1. Poppy wreathes at Lochnagar Crater.
2. Memorial to the Barnsley Pals in Sheffield Memorial Park, Serre.
3. Commonwealth War Graves' road signs at Serre.
4. Serre Road No.2 Cemetery at Serre.

THE SPECIALIST

PIERS STORIE-PUGH MBE DL
FOUNDER OF REMEMBRANCE TRAVEL, AT SERRE

Described by Piers Storie-Pugh as the location where the Pals' Ideal died on 1 July 1916, Serre was held by the Germans until their withdrawal to the Hindenberg Line in late February 1917. Today the position of the battlefield cemeteries around Serre – Serre Road No.1, No.2, No.3, Queen's, Luke Copse, Railway Hollow and the Sheffield Memorial Park – are grim testimony to the German positional advantage here.

Piers set up Remembrance Travel for the Royal British Legion in 1985, and is a leading specialist on war cemeteries and memorials worldwide, from Belgium to Burma, The Somme to Singapore. He and his team have enabled thousands of relatives and veterans to visit the graves of the Fallen. He is one of the very few qualified guides, and is no newcomer to the volunteer or military ethos, having commanded 6th/7th (Territorial Battalion) The Princess of Wales's Royal Regiment between 1992 and 1994. Thereafter he was Deputy Commander, 2nd Infantry Brigade 1994-97 in the rank of Full Colonel.

Remembrance Travel follows in the tradition of the original organized tours of the battlefield cemeteries which began in 1927, when 150 relatives made their way to France. Such was the extent of the grief, and the need to make the pilgrimage to the battlefields, that by August the following year, 10,000 relatives alighted at Beaucourt Hamel Station, the venture having captured the public imagination.

One of the foundation pillars of The Royal British Legion, embodied in its 1921 Charter, is that it should: 'perpetuate the Memory of those who died in the Service of their Country, and promote the welfare of the women and children left by those who have fallen in our service in war, and to arrange for and assist them to visit the graves of relatives killed in war.' The Legion, founded by Field Marshal Haig, continues to offer this unique service worldwide. In addition, Remembrance Travel has for many years assisted the British Embassy, Paris and the Consulate General Lille in running the 1 July Service at Thiepval on the Somme. It is styled on The Royal British Legion Service of Remembrance and it invites all-comers, including representatives from France – a reminder of 'the eternal comradeship' established between the French and British in the Great War.

Piers Storie-Pugh in Railway Hollow Cemetery, Serre.

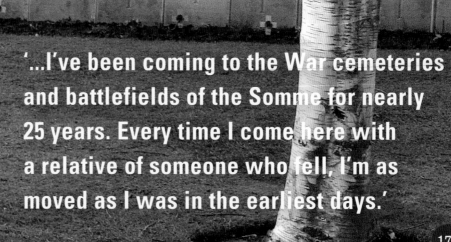

'...I've been coming to the War cemeteries and battlefields of the Somme for nearly 25 years. Every time I come here with a relative of someone who fell, I'm as moved as I was in the earliest days.'

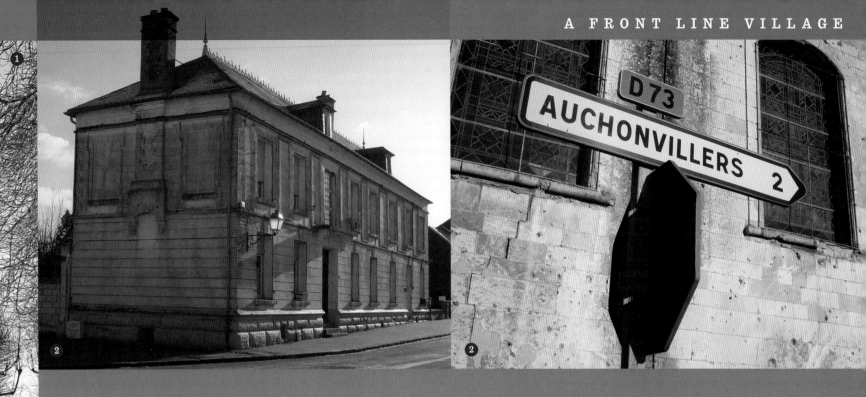

MAILLY-MAILLET

'Mailly-Maillet began at the top of the hill. There was a branch road to Auchonvillers; the main road, running straight through the town, was in the direction of Serre, which the Hun held; and a third road on the left went off to Colincamps. The town itself, though extensively damaged, had not been completely wrecked, but the few inhabitants who remained there were preparing reluctantly, under military compulsion, to leave.'

Thus Frederic Manning describes a march through the village of Mailly-Maillet on the way up to the line in 'Her Privates We', his autobiography of life as a Tommy on the Somme. William Boyd has described the book as 'the finest novel to have come out of the First World War.'

Mailly-Maillet was an important location just behind the British lines. It is one and a half miles to to Auchonvillers ("Ocean Villas" to the Tommies), and beyond that stood the old British front line of 1 July 1916. Main communication trenches began at Auchonvillers and led right up to the front at Beaumont Hamel. Mailly-Maillet served as a main billeting village for many of the troops in the area, hosting variously the 1st Lancashire

Fusiliers of the 29th Division on their arrival on the Somme from Gallipoli, the Ulstermen of the 36th Division, and latterly, Canadian troops. The original buildings which remain from the time of the war today bear testimony to the onslaught with shrapnel-pocked facades.

Like all of the villages close to the front line, Mailly-Maillet saw its share of horrors, but probably the worst was the burial of the remains of hundreds of British dead from the tragedy of 1 July, months after, in a mass grave close to the village. The grim task of 'battlefield clearance' falling to 152 Brigade of the 51st Highland Division – 'Harper's Duds' – who had taken Beaumont Hamel in the battle of the Ancre in November.

1. The old Café Jourdain.
2, 3. Views of Mailly-Maillet

173

2 3 4

'...I'm filling up now... all those people that came here, those fantastic talented people with such fantastic futures, wiped out in a second by just one bullet, and that, that's the tragedy of it all to me.'

Today Mailly-Maillet, is a sleepy village that has been largely rebuilt. The surface traces of shrapnel however, conceal an interesting past. The village is criss-crossed by a tunnel system that link back to the ex-Café Jourdain. One tunnel, bricked up by New Zealand Engineers during a period of occupying the village, led from the cellar to the local Chateau, originally a monastery, which was being used as a divisional headquarters.

The old café, whose history extends beyond the war, is now owned by a British couple, Rod and Jackie Bedford of Battlefield Experience Tours. During the war it played a pivotal role in the life of the village. It has been part *estaminet* and billeting house. It continues its Great War connections by being one of several B&Bs in the area servicing the battlefield tourist circuit.

The Bedfords continue to uncover traces of the building's past. As a bar, Rene Jourdain originally owned it from 1910. In 1914,

the Germans occupied Mailly-Maillet for a few months before they withdrew at Christmas of that year.

Further tantalising glimpses of the past have manifested themselves in the discovery of old medieval coins, buttons, little tobacco tins and the old brass sign of the café. Official village records reveal that the Lancashire Fusiliers were billeted in Mailly-Maillet at the start of the battle, many meeting their fate at Sunken Lane on 1 July.

Having spent a number of years moving around the UK, the Bedfords now consider themselves to have put down family roots in France. Jackie has spent periods of her career in both the British Army and British Police Force. They moved from the UK to realise a rural idyll in the place that former soldier Rod had fallen in love with on a visit many years before. They now host visitors from all over the world.

1. Jackie Bedford.
2, 3, 4. Views of Mailly-Maillet.

1,2. The 29th Division Memorial, by the entrance of Newfoundland Memorial Park. Battalions of the 29th suffered horrendously in their attack on Beaumont Hamel on 1 July and losses within the Division were among the worst on the First Day.

The 1st Newfoundland attacked with 752 men. Of these, 684 became casualties. Most of them were killed by machine-gun. 1st King's Own Scottish Borderers sustained losses of 552 men, and the Public Schools Battalion 522 men.

NEWFOUNDLAND MEMORIAL PARK

3. View of the trenches, looking roughly in the direction of Auchonvillers. A main communication trench ran from here all the way through to Auchonvillers, some one and a half miles distant.

4. The Caribou in the November mist of the Somme. The work of the English sculptor Basil Gotto, it looks out towards the German wire and the ground on which the Newfoundlanders died. At the base of the mound is the Memorial to the Missing of Newfoundland.

The decimation on 1 July of the Newfoundland Regiment in the attack on Beaumont Hamel precipitated its people and government after the war to buy most of the land across which the fated battalion had attacked, and to leave the ground in its war-time state for posterity. The consequence is that Newfoundland Memorial Park is one of the few remaining examples of trench systems on the Western Front. On the Pilgrimage in 1928, visitors to the trenches found that it still contained duckboards, and were able to photograph themselves wearing tin helmets and holding broken rifles that they had picked up on the battlefield. Even in the late 1960s, on his first visit to the Park, the historian Nigel Cave recalls finding 'the odd helmet and half-rusted away tin of bully beef". The Park was officially opened by Earl Haig in 1925, and it contains a number of memorials and cemeteries created to the memory of the men who died in the two principal attacks on Beaumont Hamel – which happened to be on the opening day of the Somme, and, practically speaking, the closing of it. Possibly the most conspicuous monument is the Caribou, the emblem of the Newfoundland Regiment. Described as 'seemingly baying for its young', it is a poignant and powerful symbol. Newfoundland Park is close by Hawthorn Ridge Crater, site of the premature mine detonation that famously opened the battle of the Somme. Just beyond this is another well-known location – The Sunken Lane, where the men of the 1st Lancashire Fusiliers were filmed by Malins just before Zero Hour on that first morning.

THE CURATOR

ARLENE KING, DIRECTOR OF NEWFOUNDLAND MEMORIAL PARK

'I have a passion and desire to have people understand that this was a very complex war. It wasn't as simple as men going over the top and being butchered because the generals didn't know what they were doing…'

1. Panorama of Newfoundland Memorial Park.
2,3. Arlene King, the Director of the Visitor Centre.

'It was the war widows in Newfoundland who wanted to buy the land as their way of commemorating their men… It was fascinating to arrive on the Somme and have people express concern about me being female…I've had people worrying about me being female on other levels, but never as the director of an historic site!'

The Visitor Centre at Newfoundland Park immediately locates a sense of the homeland of the men of Newfoundland who died here on 1 July. It is built using the materials and in the style of a Newfoundland fishing village, and is discreetly positioned away from the sacred ground where the men of 29th Division died. The Visitor Centre's director is Arlene King, a Newfoundland woman who was previously Director of Historic Sites in Canada.

Whilst acknowledging that people were taken aback by the appointment of a woman to set up and run a Great War visitor centre, her background in conservation, preservation and presentation have led to her creating a substantial addition to the Somme experience. Before the Centre opened, annual visitors to the Park numbered up to 10,000 annually, but since 2001 attendances have risen dramatically to almost 200,000, and Arlene recognizes that she now has to balance the interests of the visitors with the preservation aspects of the Park.

Arlene considers it an important part of her role to communicate to visitors the complexity of the Great War, and that the simplistic 'lions led by donkeys' notion has to be overcome. She considers that the role of Great War interpretation is key in developing a more realistic appreciation of what happened 90 years ago. 'Yes, it was a tragedy, but you have to consider the lack of communications, the munitions that failed, the information the Germans had captured ahead of time. That's what *Interpretation* does – it gives you all sides of the story, so you can get a perpective on it, and challenge it.'

THE OLD RAILWAY STATION, BEAUCOURT-SUR-ANCRE

Colonel Bernard Freyberg of the Royal Naval Division won his VC here at Beaucourt. As part of the 13 November attacks by the Ancre, the Royal Naval Division were to advance parallel to the line of the railway and the river, taking the village of Beaucourt, to a position just beyond it. Freyberg's Battalion, Hood, was on the right flank, by the river, and at first made good progress, following the creeping barrage up to the sidings yard of the old station. However, they then encountered stubborn German resistance. On their left, Hawke Battalion's attack had stalled completely, with losses of over 400 men inside half an hour. Freyberg rallied his troops and personally led his Hoods onto 'a pell-mell attack' on the shattered ruins of the station – their first objective.

With this renewed spirit, Hood Battalion surged into the defences at the station and held their ground until reinforcements arrived later in the day. The Division's eventual objectives – German positions east of Beaucourt – were finally taken in a renewal of the attack the next morning, Freyberg again in the vanguard. By his dashing and courageous actions he had turned the fortunes of the fight, and had been instrumental in the capture of the whole village. It was almost the final act of the campaign that had seen so much horror, and so much heroism.

In August 1928, an army of a different kind arrived on the site of these momentous events of twelve years previous. On 6 and 7 August, over 10,000 British pilgrims arrived at the newly-rebuilt Beaucourt Hamel Station. At intervals of 15 minutes they came, each train packed with 500 mourners. Amongst this enormous number of grieving relatives were many veterans – 'I wonder if my blinkin' leg is still up there?', one of them was heard to joke. From the station sidings they were taken by charabanc to the many battlefield cemeteries of the area. Many of them wandered off alone, anxious to immerse themselves into the landscape that had kept their men, before looking to commune, at last, with their dead.

1. CWGC road sign to the Ancre British Cemetery.
2. The Pilgrims of 1928 arriving on the Somme.
3. The sidings at the old Railway Station, Beaucourt-sur-Ancre, location of Hood Battalion's successful attack in the battle of the Ancre, and alighting point of 10,000 pilgrims in 1928.

THE ENTREPRENEUR

PHILIPPE FERET, HELICO-SOMME AND THE OLD RAILWAY STATION, BEAUCOURT-SUR-ANCRE

1. Philippe Feret.
2,3,4. Signs of change at the old station.
5. Alighting point for the pilgrims.

Trains no longer stop at the tiny station on the banks of the River Ancre – though the Orient Express does pass through every week. It has a new owner, and one who is aware of its historical significance in the Somme Campaign. Monsieur Philippe Feret was originally a photographer who kindled his interest and enthusiasm for the Great War by taking aerial pictures of the trenches. His passion and entrepreneurial spirit developed from there. He has bought the old station, and he also offers tourists the unique opportunity to fly over the Somme battlefields in his helicopter tours – Helico-Somme. As for the station, his vision is for it to take its place on the Circuit of Remembrance. Despite Freyberg's actions in contributing to the British Army's success at Beaucourt (and his subsequent rise to prominence), little is acknowledged in the locality. Down the road from the station stands the Ancre Cemetery, but this is only an occasional detour for

'...I have respect for the British soldiers who died for France – mort pour La France...'

coaches on their way from Newfoundland Park to The Ulster Tower. The old Railway Station, and the Royal Naval Division Memorial in Beaucourt-sur-Ancre, are largely bypassed by the essentially 1 July tourist route. One only needs to get a little way off the beaten track to uncover an important piece of Somme history. Philippe's vision is transforming the station into a museum honouring the exploits of Freyberg and the Royal Naval Division, and, recognizing the British who visit, has made part of the station an English Tea Rooms – an acknowledged echo of Faulkes' novel, 'Birdsong'. He sees that the Somme is important to the British people, and is full of admiration for the British visitors who keep alive the sacrifice of 1916 – 'mort pour La France', as Philippe says. Conversion work at the station is under way, and the Museum will open soon – the Tea Rooms are already serving "Tetley and Yorkshire in a tea pot".

1

2

Such was the destruction and chaos on the battlefield that of the 1200 men buried in Connaught Cemetery, over half were unable to be identified.

THE SCHWABEN REDOUBT

The Schwaben Redoubt will forever be associated with the 'glorious feat of arms' carried out on 1 July by the 36th (Ulster) Division. Four VCs were won in the 36th Division that day in astonishing acts of courage and heroism, by Billy McFadzean, Eric Bell, Geoffrey St George Shillington Cather and Robert Quigg. The Ulstermen successfully captured the German frontline at the Schwaben Redoubt – the only soldiers, in fact, north of the Albert-Bapaume road to take any part of the German lines. However, in the afternoon they were subjected to fierce German counter-attacks and were eventually forced to withdraw under cover of darkness. Many of their dead are buried in the Connaught and Mill Road Cemeteries close by. Because of

the location of Mill Road Cemetery – directly on the Schwaben – many of its headstones are laid flat, a legacy of the warren of tunnels causing surface subsidence. The Schwaben Redoubt was taken in the later stages of the Somme campaign, mainly by the troops of the 18th (Eastern) Division, following through their successful assault on Thiepval. The attack was launched from the southeastern edge of Schwaben Redoubt to take the eastern side, rather than the 1 July direction of the Ulstermen. 11th (Northern) Division attacked alongside the right of the 18th. After success in taking Bulgar Trench, fighting descended into a desperate attack and counter-attack which continued

1. View of Mill Road Cemetery, from the 18th Division Memorial across at Thiepval.
2. Sunrise over the Schwaben Redoubt.
3. View from the top of the Thiepval Memorial looking across to Schwaben Redoubt and the Ulster Tower. Thiepval wood is on the left middle distance. The sweep of land around the wood was No Man's Land on 1 July. The 36th Ulsters attacked out of the wood straight onto the Schwaben; the corner of Thiepval Wood visible in the picture marked the Ulsters' boundary with the Salford Pals in 32nd Division, who attacked up the hill towards the position of the camera.

for several days. In this period the 18th Division fought itself to a standstill, but held the position, despite German counter-attacks using trench mortar, gas and flame-thrower (flammenwerfer). They were relieved by the 39th Division, who took a further nine days to finally clear the whole position. The Schwaben Redoubt is undoubtedly the unmarked grave of hundreds of soldiers, both British and German, whose bodies could never be found in the churned up carnage that the Schwaben had become. That October, right through into November, the gruesome task of clearing the battlefield of bodies continued, until no more could be found.

3

THE CUSTODIAN
TEDDY COLLIGAN, THE ULSTER MEMORIAL TOWER

The focus of Northern Irish Remembrance, and their national war memorial, is the Ulster Memorial Tower, which stands within a copse of trees on the Schwaben Redoubt. It is a copy of Helen's Tower in County Down, on the Clanboye estate of the Marquis of Dufferin and Ava, where the 36th Ulsters trained before coming out to the Somme. Built in 1921, it became the first official memorial to be established along the Western Front, and during that decade its visitors averaged 400 per day. After the Second World War, however, there were many years of neglect, but the cultural importance of the sacrifice on the Schwaben was recognized again, and the Tower and its grounds were revitalized, with Princess Alice rededicating the Tower in 1991, on the 75th Anniversary of the Ulsters going over.

In 1994 the Somme Association was established under Royal Patronage, and took over upkeep of the Tower and grounds. Its remit is to extend research into the whole of Ireland's part in the Great War, as part of the ongoing peace process in Ireland, and to help provide a "common heritage" base for the Protestant and Catholic traditions to come together.

A Visitor Centre, including a café and toilet facilities was opened at the Ulster Tower on 1 July 1994. The current guardians are Teddy and Phoebe Colligan – a proposed two-week tenure looking after the Visitor Centre having turned into a five year stay so far, and this has allowed Teddy in particular to indulge his Great War enthusiasm. Back home in Ulster, 1 July is strongly commemorated again, with big parades, and Teddy and Phoebe are very keen to extend a 'warm Ulster welcome' at the Tower to their fellow countrymen and foreigners alike. The wealth of information that Teddy continues to amass is now beginning to include German accounts of the conflict, which will give a more rounded and considered view of the events of 90 years ago.

DVD VIDEO

1. View through the trees to the Ulster Tower
2. Mill Road Cemetery on the Schwaben Redoubt.
3. Teddy Colligan, Guardian of the Tower.

1. The Cross of Sacrifice at the entrance to Authuille Military Cemetery.
2. The rebuilt church and houses in the main street of Authuille.
3. The Communal Memorial at Authuille. Amongst others, it commemorates Boromée Vaquette, the first man to be killed at Thiepval in the Great War.
4. The headstone of Private H Feeney, first of the Salford Pals to die on the Somme, in February 1916.

'One evening I stood there looking over the broad marshes of the Ancre and the great mass of Aveluy Wood beyond. There was a lull in the firing, and everything was still. The sun was setting; perhaps the majesty of nature had stayed for one moment the hand of the Angel of Death. The river and marshes were a sea of gold, and the trees of the wood were tinged with fire...Shadows were lengthening in the woods and on the marshes. A cool evening breeze blew gently through the graves of our dead.'

Charles Douie, 'The Weary Road', 1929

THE CEMETERY AT AUTHUILLE

The little village of Authuille, by the banks of the Ancre, was a key assembly point on the eve of the 'Big Push', with thousands of troops massing all along the banks of the river running below the heights of Thiepval down to Blighty Valley. The village was steadily shelled to destruction by the Germans in the run-up to 1 July, and thereafter, being rebuilt in the early post-war years. In the main street stands a simple communal memorial. Amongst others, it commemorates a French farmer – Boromée Vaquette, the first man to be killed at Thiepval in the Great War. Tucked discreetly by its side is a small brick structure. This is the Salford Pals Memorial, which was unveiled on 1 July 1995 by the Lancashire Fusiliers Association, the Lancashire & Cheshire Branch of the Western Front Association and the

Mayor of Authuille. Walking past the church in the direction of Aveluy, a farm road splits off to the right. Authuille Military Cemetery is down this track. It was begun in the autumn of 1915, when the British took over the sector from the French. Trench raids began, and generally the attritional temperature was raised in this hitherto quiet part of the Front. A steady toll of the men was taken, and Authuille Cemetery contains the graves of men who were killed in the heightened tension during the long run-up to 1 July. There are many men from the 32nd and 36th Divisions buried here. The first of many hundreds of Salford Pals to be killed in the Thiepval area was Private Herbert Feeney of the 15th Battalion Lancashire Fusiliers (1st Salford Pals) on 11 February 1916.

1. Michael Stedman in his 'spiritual home', Authuille Cemetery.
2. View of the cemetery, showing the marshes of the Ancre in the distance.

THE HISTORIAN

MICHAEL STEDMAN, AUTHOR, PHOTOGRAPHER, AUTHORITY ON THIEPVAL

Michael Stedman describes the cemetery at Authuille as his spiritual home. A former teacher turned author, Michael has written many books on Thiepval and the Somme. His erudition and passion for his subject, taught in the 'outdoor classroom' of the Somme battlefields, continues to enthral newcomers to the region. He first came to the Somme almost by accident, as a stand-in teacher on a school trip. A native of Salford, Michael was gripped to learn about the part his forebears played at Thiepval on 1 July. That was thirty years ago. Today, he is a familiar figure around Authuille, the location where the Salford Pals gathered on the night before the Big Push. Referred to as 'God's Own', the men from Salford suffered dreadfully at Thiepval and elsewhere, before proving their mettle during the battle of the Somme and after, in the years 1917 to 1918. In his early days as a full-time historian, Michael had the privilege to meet and interview some of the surviving Pals, and recalls their stories in his guided walking tours around Thiepval and Authuille. With his immense knowledge of the Salford Pals and so many of their characters at his fingertips, Michael is able to evoke an authentic atmosphere of that fateful night of 30 June on the banks of the Ancre, with moving personal testimonies of the events that unfolded so disastrously on 1 July.

'I regard these locations really, as a magnificent open-air classroom. It's an ideal location to bring people to...'

The Memorial to the Missing of the Somme. This view looks up to Thiepval from No Man's Land, and shows the difficult incline the Salford Pals, the Tyneside Commercials and Glasgow Tramways were faced with.

THEN AND NOW ALONG THE SOMME FRONT OF 1 JULY : FROM HAMEL TO THE LEIPZIG SALIENT

The 1 July Front from the Ancre valley at Hamel on the left, to the Leipzig Salient beyond Thiepval, on the right. The top panorama was a series of photographs taken by the British Army when they assumed control of the sector from the French in the autumn of 1915. The present-day sequence was taken from the same grid references by Michael Stedman at an observation point near Mesnil.

Poyeres Church   3 Grand arbres   Contalmaison Villa   Bazentin le Petit Wood   Contalmaison Chateau   la Boisselle   Wood

Aveluy Church   Waterlot Chimney

POZIERES VILLAGE   HIGH WOOD   LA BOISSELLE

A V E L U Y   AVELUY CHURCH

Cross-roads at
R.M.C.V.B.

British front line

Thiepval Wood

THE SCHWABEN REDOUBT

THIEPVAL CHURC

THIEPVAL WOOD

THE ULSTER TOWER

THE RIVER ANCRE

LL ROAD

Thiepval Chateau

Line of apple trees

Thiepval-Authuille Rd

POZIERES TELECOMMUNICATIONS MAST

MEMORIAL TO THE MISSING

THE LEIPZIG SALIENT

THIEPVAL VISITOR CENTRE

18TH DIVISION MEMORIAL

Thiepval Chateau

Authuilie Wood

2 Grand arbres jumeles
(now cut down)

Courcelette Chimney

MEMORIAL TO THE MISSING THE LEIPZIG SALIENT

AUTHUILLE WOOD

AUTHUILLE VILLAGE

The 1 July Front from the Memorial to the Missing at Thiepval on the left, down to Mansel Copse at Mametz, on the right. As on previous pages, the top panorama was a series of photographs taken by the British Army when they took over the sector from the French in the autumn of 1915. The present-day sequence was taken from the same grid references, again by Michael Stedman, at a point this time on Bouzincourt Ridge, where some commanders watched the attacks on 1 July unfold.

Montauban   Wood X22,c   Willow Patch x27, d4·8   Maricourt Wood   Maricourt   Bécourt Wood   Fricourt

Tree along Peronne Road

BERNAFAY WOOD
MONTAUBAN CHURCH   THE WILLOW PATCH   BECOURT WOOD   MANSEL COPSE (MAMETZ)

THE MAYOR

MME POTIE, MAYOR OF THIEPVAL

'War to me is an atrocious word, and we should use all force to prevent it...'

By the end of 1916, Thiepval, like all the front line villages, was a destroyed wasteland. At the end of the war, the French government considered declaring the Somme battlefields a national memorial, and leaving the land exactly as it had been ravaged, as at Verdun. At Thiepval, plans for a national forest were discussed. However, populations began to return to the devastated areas soon after the fighting stopped. Agricultural work was again under way in 1919, but it was to be 20 years before the massive rebuilding programme was completed. Thiepval church was eventually rebuilt in 1930 – by which time, of course, the construction of the Memorial to the Missing was well under way.

Mme Potie's father became the mayor of the rebuilt village during the Second World War, but she is able to recall her great-grandmother's stories from the 1870 Franco-Prussian war, and she has a veritable treasure trove of documents and photos that chart the history of the village prior to the Great War, and after. Mme Potie believes that War should be prevented at all costs, and that we should learn the lessons of the past.

For her part, if she can contribute to raising the profile of Thiepval, people will learn of what happened there. Mme Potie is sure, though, that awareness of her tiny village is far greater in the UK than in France, particularly because of the number of visitors to the Memorial of the Missing – many of them British school children. She describes the awe and fascination of the children when they come face to face with the Memorial, and the reverence and respect they show for the men who lost their lives there.

1. Thiepval church, before the Great War.
2 Mme Potie, Mayor of Thiepval.
3. Thiepval Chateau, before the Great War.
4. Site of Thiepval Chateau, after the Somme.
5. The inauguration of the Memorial to the Missing, 1932.

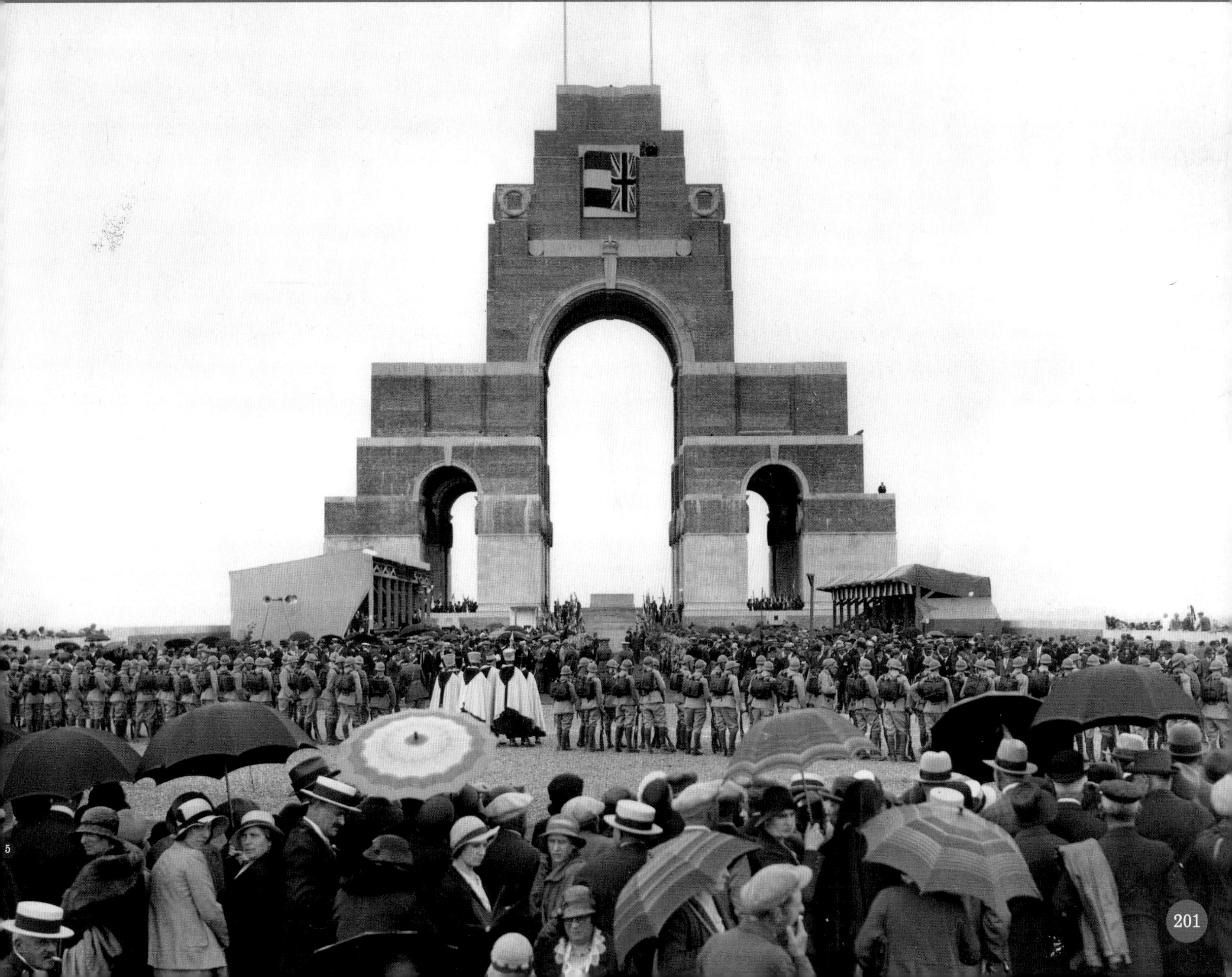

5

THE THIEPVAL VISITOR CENTRE

'...at lunch...I sort of asked why there were no explanations about what happened here, and to be fair, why there were no facilities for the thousands of visitors that come here each year.'

THE VISIONARY
SIR FRANK SANDERSON OBE

Standing within the Visitor Centre he was largely responsible for creating, Sir Frank Sanderson acknowledges the kind generosity of donors, the support of the Conseil General de la Somme, and the Historial de la Grande Guerre of Peronne, and the fact that a building exceeding his original vision now stands in the shadow of the Memorial to the Missing. The absence of any facilities at the Memorial to the Missing of the Somme, which receives over 200,000 visitors every year – a good proportion of them schoolchildren – drove Sir Frank to investigate the possibility of providing something educational. The result, after several years' hard work, has been the establishment of a visitor centre that has met with universal acclaim. The exhibition graphically and cinematically contextualizes the events at Thiepval within the Somme campaign, then in turn within the larger picture of the Great War. The aftermath is then examined – civic grief, Remembrance and the building of the Memorial to the Missing. One of the panels in the permanent exhibition has inadvertently become the *leitmotif* of the exhibition. Comprising family portraits of 600 of The Missing, its stark visual character produces an emotional response that locates one of the essential functions behind the Centre's existence. To explain, graphically, what happened here.

1,2. Construction of the Visitor Centre.
3,4. Interior views of the Centre today.
5. Exterior of the Centre as landscaping got under way.
6. Guillaume de Fonclere, Director of the Historial de la Grande Guerre, Péronne.
7. Sir Frank Sanderson OBE

THE MUSEUM DIRECTOR
GUILLAUME DE FONCLARE

'...Great War interpretation...helps to define the *reality* of what war really is and means.'

The newly-appointed Director of the Historial de la Grande Guerre in Péronne, Guillaume de Fonclare, is charged with the major task of the presentation of The Great War in the Somme region, and the Thiepval Visitor Centre, which will now come under the jurisdiction of the Historial, has assumed a significant importance for him, not least by the nature of its exhibition. Whilst the Historial is an historical research centre, the Visitor Centre at Thiepval is concerned with Remembrance of the British *and* French sacrifice. Its experience is about time, place and people, and attempts to get near to a living history. It does not rely on traditional museum formulas of exhibits and artefacts to deliver its key messages, so therefore is able to complement the Historial.

Guillaume welcomes this new direction in Great War *interpretation*, especially with regard to the young students of the subject, and particularly so on the 90th anniversary of the Battle of the Somme – the Somme is now passing from memory into history, with the demise of the last few survivors. Guillaume hopes to develop the Historial into a major landmark on the Somme, and stress the common heritage that France and Britain share in this part of the world.

Pozières sits on the highest point of the battlefields and formed a key part of the German Second Position, the backbone of their defences on the Somme.

POZIERES

1. The Australian 1st Division Memorial, taken from the nearby viewing platform. The 'back door' route across the ridge to Thiepval is plainly seen from this position.

There are certain locations on the Somme battlefields that will always be associated with the divisions that fought there. Pozières is one such place, for it will always be linked with the supreme sacrifice made by thousands of Australians who fought and died in one of the most extended and bloody attritional actions of the Great War. Pozières was strategically of great importance, for it occupied a key part of the German Second Position, which ran all along the high ground of Thiepval Ridge southeast down to Guillemont and Ginchy, on the way to the River Somme. If the Allies could take Pozières, then a 'back door' into Thiepval would have been opened. The village itself was reduced to rubble in the struggle – it was alternately shelled intensely by both sides as possession shifted from the Germans to the Australians and British. The Australians suffered an horrendous scale of casualties – almost 23,000 in two months, as they ground their way through Pozières and onto Mouquet Farm ("Moo Cow Farm" to the Aussies, "Mucky Farm" to the Tommies).

Their courage and heroics amidst this extremely bitter fighting are commemorated today by the graceful obelisk of the 1st Australian Division Memorial, located on the west side of Pozières, by the Albert-Bapaume road. In 1993 a bronze bas-relief plaque was added to the Memorial entrance. Opposite the Memorial are the remains of 'Gibraltar', a German OP blockhouse. During the fighting for Pozières, this was reputed to be the only structure left standing in the entire village. In front of this is a viewing platform, which gives impressive views of the Memorial and Thiepval in the distance.

Further along the road to Albert is the large Pozières British Cemetery and Memorial, which commemorates the soldiers who died during the 1918 German Spring Offensive. 14,600 names are inscribed around the walls – which form the Memorial (to the Missing), and 2,700 men are buried in the Cemetery.

1

THE COLLECTOR

DOMINIQUE ZANARDI, PROPRIETOR OF LE TOMMY BAR, POZIÈRES

'...the name of the soldier from the First World War, a very popular name, the best – everybody knows who is Tommy.'

Dominique Zanardi, the proprietor of Le Tommy Bar in Pozières, is a collector. He collects every conceivable form of artefact and detritus from the battlefields all around. He has done this since he was 12, when he realized he could sell the lead shrapnel that he'd gathered from the fields surrounding his home. After his schoolwork was done, he would be seen diligently combing the fields. His legendary hauls eventually caught the attention of some British Great War enthusiasts who took it upon themselves to tutor the young Dominique on the war over a meal – at their expense.

He has been hooked ever since on any scrap of information or physical thing to do with what Dominique calls 'the biggest battle in the world'. His collection grew so extensive that he was able to put on his own exhibitions – the nucleus of the collection at the museum in Albert was his. In 1996, he seized the opportunity to buy the bar on the main street of Pozieres, in which he intended to tell the story of the 'biggest battle in the world' in his very singular and individual way, and every year since then, the number of visitors to the legendary Le Tommy have grown, and now large coach parties – usually of British schoolchildren – arrive at a rate of up to 10 a day. The bubblegum machines dispensing shrapnel balls proving to be as popular with them as the egg and chips.

As a repository of the detritus of war, Le Tommy bar is without equal, and the garden at the rear is testimony to this. Dominique has constructed a complete trench system – both British and German. His most recent acquisitions though are possibly his most sinister – he has procured some British manufactured TNT bricks of 1915 vintage – of the type that would have been used for the Hawthorn Ridge Mine on 1 July 1916.

1,2,3. Dominique Zanardi.
4. Detail of the trenches in the rear of Le Tommy.
5,6,7. Great War gun, and the 'Iron Harvest', some of the huge quantities of shells and shell cases that Dominic collects.
8. One of Le Tommy Bar's Tommies that stand sentry by the front door.

LE TOMMY BAR

Albert JACKA, VC
1893 - 1932

Gallipoli
1915

Pozières
1916

Bullecourt
1917

Messines
1917

14th Battalion
A.I.F.

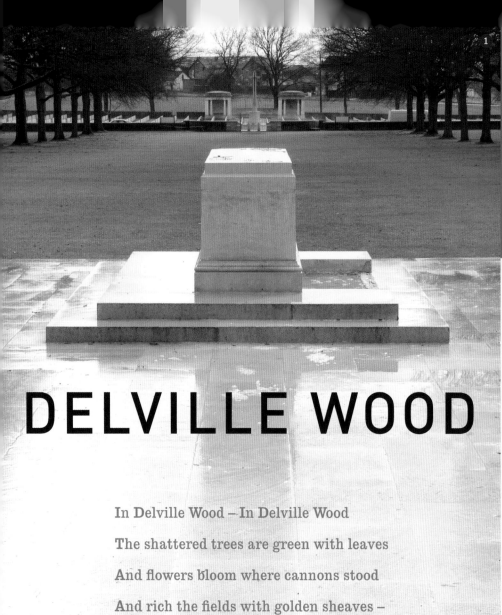

DELVILLE WOOD

In Delville Wood – In Delville Wood

The shattered trees are green with leaves

And flowers bloom where cannons stood

And rich the fields with golden sheaves –

Sleep soft ye dead, for God is good –

And peace has come to Delville Wood

Lt. FC Cornell

Delville Wood is the South African National War Memorial. It also commemorates those South Africans who died in the Second World War and in Korea, as well as the sacrifice made by the South African Brigade on the Somme. The Memorial was raised in South Africa by public subscription, and was inaugurated in 1926. On 11 November 1986, a new museum was opened within the grounds. The oak trees which now line the walkway to the Memorial were grown from acorns brought from Cape Colony. In the wood immediately behind the Memorial stands an old hornbeam – the only tree to survive the devastation wrought in Delville Wood in the summer of 1916.

The large Delville Wood Cemetery is across the road from the Memorial. There are 5493 graves, and a testimony to the horrific nature of the fighting is that two-thirds of them remain Unknown. When the new museum was built in the 1980s, the remains of three soldiers were discovered, although logistically, Delville Wood must still bear the remains of many more soldiers underneath its trees.

1. The Great War Stone at Delville Wood, looking towards the Cemetery.
2. Inauguration of the Delville Wood South African Memorial, 1926.
3. The Hornbeam – the only tree in Delville Wood to survive the destruction.
4. Delville Wood Cemetery.

The large Delville Wood Cemetery is across the road from the Memorial. There are 5,493 graves, and a testimony to the horrific nature of the fighting is that two-thirds of them remain Unknown.

'Some of the battle orders for the first battle of the Somme read: 'the objective of the patrol this evening is to kill the bosch and blow out his dugouts...'

THE PROFESSIONAL
ROD BEDFORD, BATTLEFIELD TOUR GUIDE

Rod Bedford joined the Army when he was 15 years old, and served in the Grenadier Guards from 1970 until 1989. During his period of service he was an instructor at Sandhurst for two years, then served in Northern Ireland. His father is a veteran of World War Two and the Korean War. After 19 years in the Army, Rod joined the Kent Police Force, and the visits to the Somme battlefields during his army days were the beginning of a passion that led him back there years later, in an off-duty police motorcycle cavalcade. It was the first Battlefield Tour he hosted. Ironically enough, all the bikes were BMWs. Soon after, mindful of the age of his daughters – young enough to settle into a French primary school – and the pursuit of a rural ideal, Rod took the opportunity of leaving the Kent Police and moving to the Somme. The Bedfords arrived in Mailly-Maillet in 2000.

Today, the self-confessed "storyteller" devours any books he can get on the battle of the Somme and the Great War, and has amassed an encyclopaedic knowledge. Rod regales his Battlefield tourists with these stories, often presenting conflicting views of the same battle, and always adding little-known facts and figures. One of the most absorbing aspects of Rod's analysis of a battle, however, comes from his own experience as a soldier. *Combat appreciation* is second nature to a soldier in a conflict situation, and determines his responses in achieving his objectives. By the hornbeam in Delville Wood, Rod explains how, after the tragedy of 1 July, the British Army's learning curve led to the combat appreciation skills still in use in the British Army of today.

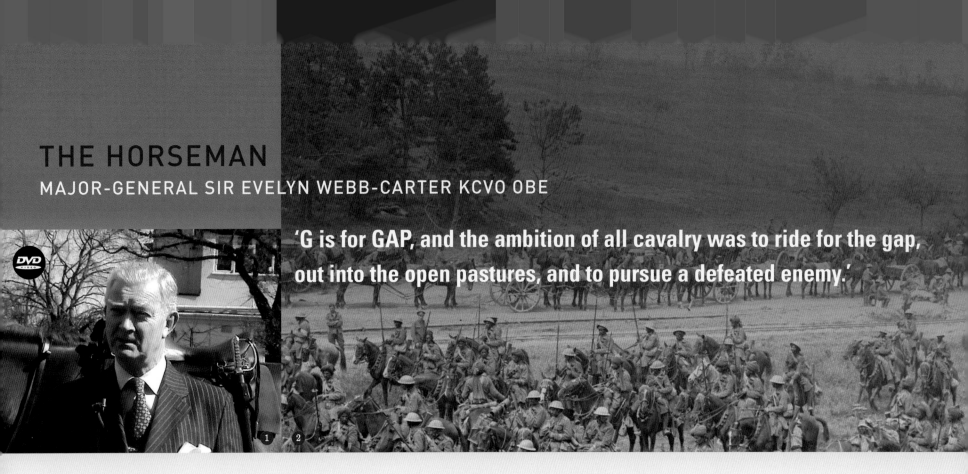

THE HORSEMAN
MAJOR-GENERAL SIR EVELYN WEBB-CARTER KCVO OBE

'G is for **GAP**, and the ambition of all cavalry was to ride for the gap, out into the open pastures, and to pursue a defeated enemy.'

Evelyn Carter-Webb was commissioned into the Grenadier Guards in 1966, and retired from the Army in 2001 to take up the appointment of Controller of the Army Benevolent Fund. He is Colonel of the Duke of Wellington's Regiment, and also Honorary Regimental Colonel of the King's Troop, Royal Horse Artillery. At St John's Wood Barracks, he analyses the attack on High Wood.

With the conflict thus far dominated by trench warfare, Haig at last saw the opportunity to take and hold High Wood by using cavalry. High Wood had been evacuated by the Germans after the successful advance of the Dawn Attack on 14 July. Unfortunately the logistics of moving up the cavalry squadrons to their starting positions took most of the day, and by the time of the charge, the wood had been re-occupied by the German defenders, who lay in wait for the advancing cavalry in hidden positions both within the wood and the corn fields around it. Finally, the cavalry charged, with lances couched, and they did in fact take 32 Germans prisoner, but many of the men and their mounts were killed by machine-gun, and Haig's longed for breakout into open ground did not materialize.

With the leaps of technology in this, the first true industrial war, the machine-gun, heavy artillery, railways, and of course the tank (the *iron cavalry*), greatly reduced the opportunities available to exploit the cavalry's strengths in this and future actions. The traditional tactic of 'breaking the G' – with the success of which the mounts could enjoy 'good sport' – and which had been deployed effectively since the days of Alexander the Great, had all but come to an end.

VERY GALLANT GENTLEMAN

1932

UNDERNEATH HERE LIES AN OLD HORSE. CALL'D WONDER FROM HIS EXTRAORDINARY AGE BEING FORTY YEARS OLD WHEN HE DIED.

1. Major-General Sir Evelyn Webb-Carter at St. John's Wood Barracks, London.
2. Cavalry waiting to move up to High Wood, 14 July 1916.
3. Captain Nick Parker with Kemp.
4,5. Headstones of revered horses at St. John's Wood Barracks.

'...the fighting spirit, and the tenacity and the raw courage of the British Soldier; that makes me terribly proud of my regiment, the Durham Light Infantry.'

THE SOLDIER

BRIGADIER TIM GREGSON MBE, BRITISH MILITARY ATTACHÉ, PARIS

The Butte de Warlencourt, marked the extent of the Allied advance in the Battle of the Somme. With its strange, gleaming white appearance, prominent on the landscape, it was said to mesmerize the Allied troops: '...it had become an obsession. Everybody wanted it. It loomed large in the minds of the soldiers in the forward area and they attributed many of their misfortunes to it...So it had to be taken. It seems that the attack was one of those tempting, and unfortunately frequent, local operations which are so costly and which are rarely worthwhile.' These were the views of Lieutenant-Colonel Roland Boys Bradford, Commanding Officer of the 9th Durham Light Infantry (DLI), after his men's attack on the Butte.

The DLI – the 'Gateshead Ghurkas' – had, in fact, succeeded in taking the position, but a determined counter-attack gradually pushed them back. They lost over 400 men, and the British only took hold of the Butte after the German withdrawal the following spring. Wooden crosses in memory of all the men who fell were erected on top of the mound. One was to the 9th DLI. It held the inscription "Dulce et decorum est pro patria mori" – it is sweet and fitting to die for one's country.

The Butte de Warlencourt was purchased by The Western Front Association and a permanent memorial has now been erected. Standing next to the Memorial on the summit, Brigadier Tim Gregson recalls the tenacity and dedication to duty of the men of the North-East who took, but could not keep, this position. He is the Deputy Colonel of the Durham Light Infantry, and is drawn to this evocative location which stills holds a grim significance in Durham folklore. As British Military Attaché in France, Brigadier Gregson's duties every so often bring him back to the Great War. The remains of British Tommies continue to be discovered along the Western Front, and it is Brigadier Gregson's task to oversee the re-interment of the remains into a permanent, marked grave. It is, for him, yet another poignant reminder of the sacrifice these men made during the conflict.

1. Road sign on the Albert-Bapaume road, showing the extent of the front in November 1916.
2. Brigadier Tim Gregson on the summit of the Butte de Warlencourt.

THE WESTERN FRONT
ASSOCIATION

BUTTE de WARLENCOURT
MEMORIAL

This ancient artificial mound, the Butte de Warlencourt,
marks the limit of the British advance
in the Battle of the Somme in 1916. Dominating the battlefield,
it was strongly fortified by the Germans
and withstood successive fierce attacks
by the British 47th, 9th and 50th Divisions in October and November.
On the German retreat to the Hindenburg Line in February 1917
it passed into British hands, only to be retaken
in the German offensive of March 1918.
On the 25th August 1918, during the final Allied offensive,
it was reoccupied by the British 21st Division without opposition.

This memorial was unveiled by John Terraine, President of the WFA,
on June 30th 1990, in the presence of the Souvenir Français-Arras Sector,
officials and members of the Commune of Warlencourt,
and members of the Western Front Association.

It marks the acquisition of this historic site by the WFA
in remembrance of the Battle of the Somme.

THE GENEALOGISTS

KEN AND PAM LINGE, ORIGINATORS OF 'THE MISSING OF THE SOMME' DATABASE AT THIEPVAL

Over the past few years our initial interests in family history and the local men who served and died in the Great War has developed into something more wide ranging. When we heard that a Visitor Centre was to be built at Thiepval we saw the opportunity for the Centre to collate and display photographs and biographical details of the men commemorated on the Thiepval Memorial.

We created The Missing of the Somme database as a means of accessing the information collected. Information is taken initially from the online Commonwealth War Graves Commission (CWGC) Debt of Honour Register. This register shows name, rank, regiment, serial number, date of death and place of burial and commemoration. If age and family details were supplied to CWGC by the next of kin these details will also be included. In the case of non-commissioned soldiers this information is further supplemented with details of places of birth, residence and enlistment and any former regiment. Such detail is found in the publication Soldiers Died in the Great War (SDGW) which is also available as a CD-Rom; a web version has recently been made available which allows information to be downloaded for a fee.

An excellent source of additional information is the obituaries printed in the many regional newspapers of the period which often also provide the only surviving picture. These can contain a great deal of personal information such as dates of enlistment and deployment, details of past injuries, copies of letters to the family as well as education and employment details, names of next of kin and information on siblings who served. Microfilm copies of such papers are usually kept in local libraries or alternatively may be held at the British Library's Newspaper archives at Colindale, North London.

Rolls of Honour produced after the war are another valuable resource. Such rolls were sometimes produced by schools, employers and local towns and villages and often contain pictures of the Fallen. Again local libraries will normally keep copies of such books pertaining to their area. Otherwise both the British Library and the Imperial War Museum have extensive collections in their reading rooms in London. University libraries (such as the Bodleian in Oxford) may also hold copies. Catalogues of library collections are often available to be searched online. Other information can be found in school magazines, school rolls and trade magazines, for example Great Western Railway magazine contains details of their employees' service. More recently there have also been a great number of books published relating to local war memorials as well as those providing background information on individual battles and regiments. There are also a number of websites which provide access to similar information.

Interest in genealogy has rekindled an interest in the Great War from many people who, like us, want to understand what happened to their relatives. Even after some 90 years there is still a wealth of information to be found and we thank those people who have generously shared their information with us. Through photographs, biographical information and letters these brave men become more than names on memorials, they become once again sons, brothers, husbands and fathers. To date "The Missing of the Somme" database holds records for a small, but growing, percentage of the 72,000 men commemorated on the Thiepval Memorial. It is updated periodically and we intend to continue to add to it for as long as new information becomes available. The database helps families provide a link to the events of the Great War and reminds us that although these men may still be "missing" they are certainly not "forgotten".

We would be pleased to receive any information, or respond to queries, on any men who are commemorated on the Memorial. Please contact us at Drystones, Heugh House Lane, Haydon Bridge, Northumberland, NE47 6ND or email pam_ken.linge@btinternet.com.

ONLINE

THE LONG LONG TRAIL
http://www.1914-1918.net/
Information and help on how to research a soldier.
A great starting point.

NATIONAL ARCHIVES
http://www.nationalarchives.gov.uk/documentsonline/
Includes Medal Index Cards, Royal Naval Seamen Records, Women's Auxiliary Corps Records also links to Victory Cross Registers and Digitised First World War Diaries.

MILITARY-GENEALOGY.COM
(NAVAL AND MILITARY PRESSES WEBSITE)
http://www.military-genealogy.com/
It includes Soldiers Died in The Great War (1914-1919), Army Roll of Honour (1939-1945) and National Roll (1914-1918)

LONDON GAZETTE ONLINE
http://www.gazettes-online.co.uk
This includes Officer Promotions and Bravery Citations

CWGC
http://www.cwgc.org/debt_of_honour

CANADIAN ARCHIVES
http://www.collectionscanada.ca
Contains Canadian Attestation Papers

AUSTRALIAN ARCHIVES
http://www.awm.gov.au/database/biographical.asp
Includes Roll of Honour, Nominal Roll, Commemorative Roll, Honours and Award and Red Cross Queries

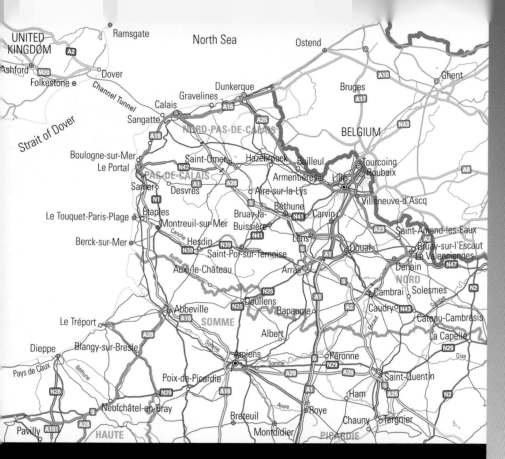

GETTING THERE

The battlefields, cemeteries and memorials of the Somme lie in the region of Picardy, and straddle the adjacent French départements of the Somme and Pas-de-Calais, to the north-east of Amiens and south-west of Arras. Both cities are accessible by train and pay-toll motorways (the A16 linking the Channel ports and Paris, and the A1 linking Calais, Lille and Paris respectively).

Apart from these major regional centres, with their abundance of hotels and restaurants to suit every budget, nearer the battlefields are the towns of Albert, Bapaume, Corbie and Peronne, each offering good facilities as a regional base for exploring the region. Undoubtedly, the region is most successfully visited by car, and is easily accessible for British visitors via ferry or the Channel Tunnel. There is an official Circuit of Remembrance.

Various companies offer organized tours of the battlefields and memorials.

The listing (right) offers a few of the best hotels and pensions in the region.

★★★ **BEST WESTERN ROYAL PICARDIE, ALBERT**
Avenue du Général Leclerc 80300 ALBERT
Telephone 03 22 75 37 00 **Fax** 03 22 75 60 19
Web www.royalpicardie.com
Email royalpicardie@wanadoo.fr
Tariffs Double rooms from €78,00-153,00
The hotel has the advantage of lying near the heart of the region. It has 24 air-conditioned rooms. The restaurant offers both regional and classic French cuisine, and there is a friendly, informal bar.

★★ **HOTEL DE LA BASILIQUE, ALBERT**
3-5, rue Gambetta 80300 ALBERT
Telephone 03 22 75 04 71 **Fax** 03 22 75 10 47
Web www.hoteldelabasilique.fr
Email hotel-de-la-basilique@wanadoo.fr
Tariffs Double rooms from €58,00-62,00
Closed for three weeks from 1 August
A town-house hotel at the centre of Albert, facing the church, and near to the Musee de la Somme and the Albert Tourist Office. Recently renovated, it offers 10 rooms, a restaurant providing local diushes with a number of house specialities, and a bar. Its central location mans that other facilities such as discos, restaurants, bowling, cinema and swimming pool are close at hand.

★★ **HOTEL DE LA PAIX, ALBERT**
43, rue Victor Hugo 80300 ALBERT
Telephone 03 22 75 01 64 **Fax** 03 22 75 44 17
Tariffs Double rooms from €44,00-70,00
Recently refurbished in a pleasant setting. You are guaranteed a warm reception, and traditional cuisine.

★★ **HOSTELLERIE DES REMPARTS**
23, rue Beaubois 80200 PERONNE
Telephone 03 22 84 01 22 **Fax** 03 22 84 31 96
Tariffs Double rooms from €70,00-95,00
A stately, old-fashioned and comfortable hotel within the walls of the old town, with an excellent restaurant offeing very high quality cuisine combining traditional recipes with local specialities. A favourite with battlefield tourists, the staff are well-versed in the subject.

★★ **HOTEL GRILL CAMPANILE, PERONNE**
Route de Paris 80200 PERONNE
Telephone 03 22 84 22 22 **Fax** 03 22 84 16 86
Email peronne@campanile.fr
Tariffs Double rooms from €39,00-54,00
Situated in the countryside just south of Peronne, this is a more economic choice, but offers traditional hotel-restaurant facilities, including a terrace restaurant, conference and banqueting rooms.

★★ **LE PRIEURE (THE PRIORY), RANCOURT**
24, route nationale 17 80360 RANCOURT
Telephone 03 22 85 04 43 **Fax** 03 22 85 06 69
Web www.hotel-le-prieure.fr
Email contact@hotel-le-prieure.fr
Tariffs Double rooms from €65,00-71,00
Lying on the rural outskirts of Peronne in the direction of Bapaume, its impressive white masonry façade faces the battlefields. Very comfortable, with a gastronomic restaurant.

AWAITING CLASSIFICATION **BEST WESTERN HOTEL-RESTAURANT LE SAINT CLAUDE, PERONNE**
42, place Louis Daudré 80200 PERONNE
Telephone 03 22 79 49 49 **Fax** 03 22 79 10 57
Email hotel.saintclaude@wanadoo.fr
Tariffs Double rooms from €95,00-100,00
In the heart of the town and near the Historial de la Grande Guerre, each room is unique, and there is a restaurant and bar.

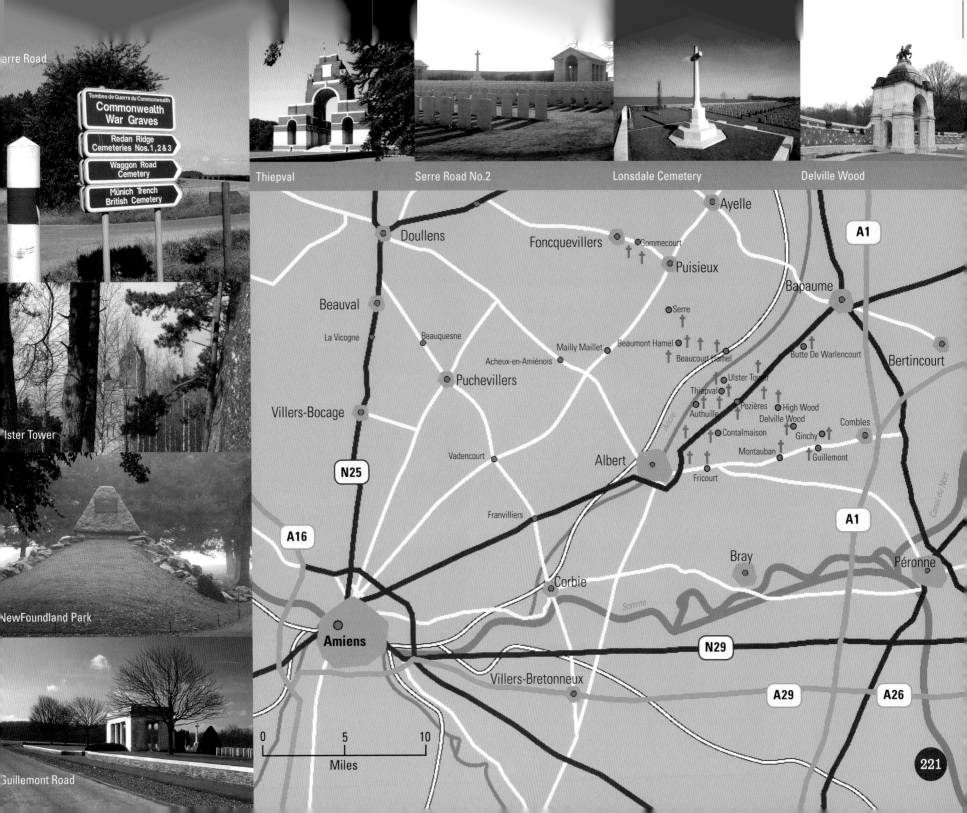

Serre Road

Commonwealth War Graves
Tombes de Guerre du Commonwealth

Redan Ridge
Cemeteries Nos. 1, 2 & 3

Waggon Road
Cemetery

Münich Trench
British Cemetery

Ulster Tower

NewFoundland Park

Guillemont Road

Thiepval

Serre Road No.2

Lonsdale Cemetery

Delville Wood

A1

Ayelle

Doullens

Foncquevillers

Gommecourt

Puisieux

Bapaume

Beauval

Serre

La Vicogne

Beauquesne

Mailly Maillet

Beaumont Hamel

Butte De Warlencourt

Bertincourt

Acheux-en-Amiénois

Beaucourt Hamel

Puchevillers

Ulster Tower

Thiepval

Pozières

High Wood

Villers-Bocage

Authuille

Delville Wood

Combles

Contalmaison

Ginchy

N25

Vadencourt

Montauban

Guillemont

Albert

Fricourt

A1

Franvilliers

A16

Bray

Péronne

Corbie

Somme

Amiens

N29

Villers-Bretonneux

A29

A26

0   5   10
Miles

ACKNOWLEDGEMENTS AND READING LIST

Our deep gratitude and thanks go first to our Historical Advisor, Michael Stedman. The steady guidance he has given us has been key to the whole project. We could not have made this book without his reliable presence, which has always been there when we needed it. For providing encouragement and practical help our thanks go to Brigadier Tim Gregson, Sir Frank Sanderson, Sian Mexsom of the ABF, Piers Storie-Pugh of the RBL, Brother Nigel Cave, and Liz Bowers of The Imperial War Museum. The task of organising and shaping our ideas and research has been undertaken by Andrew Heritage, our Editorial Consultant. His input has been invaluable.

Nobody approaching the literature on the battle of the Somme can avoid Martin Middlebrook's masterly achievement, **The First Day on the Somme**, nor Lyn McDonald's **Somme**, both available from Penguin. For detailed accounts of events and locations, individuals, battalions and divisions, the **Pen & Sword** catalogue is both exhaustive and outstanding in its breadth and depth. The many quotations from eye-witnesses which feature in this book have been drawn, with permission, from original recordings and archives held by the Imperial War Museum, some of which also appear more fully in Peter Hart's **The Somme** (Weidenfeld & Nicholson), Martin Middlebrook's **The First Day on the Somme**, and Max Arthur's **Forgotten Voices of the Great War** (Ebury Press).

Battlefield Guide to the Somme, Major and Mrs Holt; **Beaumont Hamel**, Nigel Cave; **Birdsong**, Sebastian Faulks; **Blackadder: The Whole Damn Dynasty**, Richard Curtis; **The Imperial War Museum Book of the Somme**, Malcolm Brown; **Chronicles of the Great War**, Peter Simkins; **The Dada Reader**, Dawn Ades; **Death of a Hero**, Richard Aldington; **DK World History Atlas**, ed. Jeremy Black; **First World War**, H P Willmott; **The First Day on the Somme**, Martin Middlebrook; **The First World War**, Peter Simkins; **The First World War**, John Keegan; **The First World War**, Richard Holmes; **Forgotten Victory**, Gary Sheffield; **Forgotten Voices**, Max Arthur; **From Ypres to Cambrai**, Frank Hawkins; **Goodbye to All That**, Robert Graves; **The Great War**, BBC; **Guillemont**, Michael Stedman; **Her Privates We**, Frederic Manning; **Journey's End**, RC Sheriff; **La Boisselle**, Michael Stedman; **The Landscape Vision of Paul Nash**, Roger Cardinal; **Matters of Conflict**, ed. Nicholas J Saunders; **Memoirs of George Sherston**, Siegfried Sassoon; **The Missing of the Somme**, Geoff Dyer; **Origins of the Second World War**, A J P Taylor; **The Poems of Wilfred Owen**; **Undertones of War**, Edmund Blunden; **Punch** 1914-1918; **Redan Ridge**, Michael Renshaw; **The Regeneration Trilogy**, Pat Barker; **Serre**, Jack Horsfall and Nigel Cave; **Sites of Memory, Sites of Mourning**, Jay Winter; **Somme**, Lyn Macdonald; **The Somme, the Day by Day Account**, Chris McCarthy; **The Somme**, Peter Hart; **The Somme**, Gary Sheffield; **Symbol of Courage**, Max Arthur; **Thiepval**, Michael Stedman; **Thiepval Exhibition Centre Guidebook**; **Walking the Somme**, Paul Reed.

PHOTOGRAPHIC CREDITS

INDEX

In order to retrieve information more easily, this Index is divided into three sections: a general subject and personal name index; a gazetteer of geographical names; and a summary by nationality of the military units mentioned in the book. This is not an Order of Battle, merely a listing with page references.